ABOUT THE AUTHOR

Albert Ellis was born in Pittsburgh and grew up in New York City. He holds a bachelor's degree from the City College of New York; and M.A. and Ph.D. degrees in Clinical Psychology from Columbia University. He has taught at Rutgers University and New York University; has been Chief Psychologist of the New Jersey State Diagnostic Center and later Chief Psychologist of the New Jersey Department of Institutions and Agencies; is a Consultant in Clinical Psychology to the Veterans Administration; is Executive Director of the Institute for Rational Living, Inc.; and for the last two decades has been in the private practice of psychotherapy and marriage and family counseling in New York City.

Dr. Ellis is a Fellow of the American Psychological Association, and has been President of its Division of Consulting Psychology and a Member of its Council of Representatives. He is a Fellow (and Past-President) of the Society for the Scientific Study of Sex; and a Fellow of the American Association of Marriage Counselors, the American Sociological Association, and the American Association for the Advancement of Science. He has been Vice-President of the American Academy of Psychotherapists; Chairman of the Marriage Counseling Section of the National Council on Family Relations; and a member of the Executive Committee of the American Association of Marriage Counselors, Psychologists in Private Practice, Psychologists Interested in the Advancement of Psychotherapy, and the New York Society of Clinical Psychologists. He has served as Associate Editor of the *Journal of Marriage and the Family*, the *International Journal of Sexology*, *Advances in Sex Research*, the *Journal of Sex Research*, and *Rational Living*.

Dr. Ellis has published over two hundred papers in psychological, psychiatric, and sociological journals, periodicals, and anthologies. He has authored or edited twenty-three books and monographs, including: *The Folklore of Sex*, *The American Sexual Tragedy*, *How to Live with a Neurotic*, *The Art and Science of Love*, *The Encyclopedia of Sexual Behavior*, *Creative Marriage*, *A Guide to Rational Living*, *Reason and Emotion in Psychotherapy*, *Sex and the Single Man*, *The Intelligent Woman's Guide to Manhunting*, *The Case for Sexual Liberty*, and *Homosexuality: Its Causes and Cure*.

Sex

Without Guilt

by

Albert Ellis, Ph.D.

Melvin Powers
Wilshire Book Company

12015 Sherman Road, No. Hollywood, CA 91605

Published by special arrangement
with Lyle Stuart—New York

Copyright © 1958 and 1966 by Albert Ellis, Ph.D.

Queries regarding rights and permissions
should be addressed to
Lyle Stuart, Inc.
at 239 Park Avenue South, N.Y., N.Y. 10003

Publishing history:
 Lyle Stuart edition
   First printing: January, 1958
   Second printing: May, 1958
   Third printing: March, 1959
   Fourth printing: April, 1963
   Fifth printing: January, 1966

 Portuguese edition: 1960
 Hillman edition: 1960
 Macfadden-Bartel edition: 1961
 Grove Press Black Cat edition: 1965
 Wilshire Book Company edition 1966

ISBN 0-87980-145-X

Printed in the United States of America

Contents

Dedicated to the countless men and women who have fought the lonely battle against guilt for doing those sexual things which are neither harmful to themselves nor to others.

Introduction

I first became aware of what *The Independent* was and what it stood for in the winter of 1955, when Paul Krassner, who was then its managing editor, and who has more recently been the editor and publisher of the uniquely iconoclastic periodical, *The Realist*, wrote to ask if I had any unpublished material in which they might be interested. He had become aware of my work in the field of sex, love, and marriage and family relations, Mr. Krassner said, when he had read my book, *The Folklore of Sex*, which the paper's bookselling di-

vision had distributed. Did I, he asked, have any articles which other periodicals had refused to print, but
which *The Independent* might be delighted to rescue
from obscurity?

It just so happened that I did have several such articles on sexual topics; and that, after reading a few issues
of this unusual monthly newspaper (then called
Exposé) which Paul Krassner sent along with his query,
I was more than willing to submit them to *The Independent*. For this periodical, which I had previously heard
about but had never seen, immediately struck me as being utterly unique in its field—a truly non-partisan
publication with no axe whatever to grind except one
that is perhaps the least seldom wielded in this presumably democratic nation: that of absolute, complete, and
unequivocal free speech.

The more I got to know about *The Independent*, and
to become familiar with the work and personality of its
publisher and editor, Lyle Stuart, the more did I realize
that perhaps never before in the annals of American
publishing has anything like this paper existed—or at
least flourished so persistently and well. Other liberal
periodicals have, of course, been extant in this country;
a few still are. But, almost invariably, these publications have beaten the drum for some political, economic, or social point of view.

Not so *The Independent*. Its one avowed purpose is
to print anything of legitimate and significant news
value that is not easily publishable elsewhere. And by
anything I mean anything. Where politically liberal

periodicals frequently have religious or sexual taboos, or where socially enlightened journals often have political or economic prejudices, *The Independent* is the only paper I know that seems to have *no* tabus or restrictions, and that publishes *all* kinds of news and fiction, no matter on whose political, economic, religious, medical, sexual, or other toes its contents may step.

This is not to say that I always agree with the editorial or other matter in *The Independent*. I don't. Its columns, like those of all liberal periodicals I know, are sometimes devoted to exaggerated or over-scarily presented attacks on certain vested interests, such as the American Medical Association, whose activities I cannot get enthusiatic about, but which I do not judge to be as nefarious as some of *The Independent's* writers do. It has also given space to a series of articles attempting to whitewash the notorious Krupp dynasty in Germany, whose viewpoint neither I nor the editor could heartily endorse.

That, however, is the uncommon virtue of *The Independent:* that it prints views, including many of my own, that Lyle Stuart by no means personally favors, but which he nonetheless feels should be given a public hearing. Perhaps there are several other modern publications which more than occasionally do this, too. If so, I cannot at the moment recall reading them.

In any event, my first reading of several copies of *The Independent* induced me to send Paul Krassner four papers which I had written on sexual topics for which I could find no publishing outlet. All these papers had been commissioned by other periodicals or book publishers, and were eagerly awaited by the commissioning editors. They were all quickly rejected, however, accompanied by apologetic notes or phone calls which explained that although they were clearly and interestingly written, their subject matter was too uncompromisingly sexual for them to appear in public print. When resubmitted to other publications, their content was found wanting for modern mass media.

Shortly after I sent these four articles to Paul Krassner he wrote me that he had shown them to Lyle Stuart and that they both felt that these were just the thing for *The Independent*: they would run them all. So they did; and so much reader interest was thereby engendered that, starting with the February 1956 issue, I became *The Independent*'s regular columnist—the only sex columnist, I daresay, writing for any American newspaper.

My road as a columnist for *The Independent* has not been totally unrocky. Thick and fast comments on my commentaries began shortly after I began writing, and all have hardly been favorable. Of the more than thirty letters regarding my articles that have thus far been published in the paper, almost two thirds have been savagely negative. Icy salutes, for example, such as these:

From a man in Harper Woods, Michigan: "Please cancel my subscription at once. It is not the kind of reading matter we want to have coming into our home. With all the important matters to write about nowadays, you publish some nonsensical stuff; especially that article on masturbation."

From a correspondent in Daytona Beach, Florida: "Dr. Ellis is a materialistic hedonist of a low-grade Epicurean type. I say 'low-grade' because the classical Epicurean was more discriminating and restrained in his search for pleasure."

From a woman in San Francisco: "It seems pitiful that a young man such as you should delude yourself that you are doing mankind a service in printing all the foul mouthings of men who have been unable to break into print elsewhere."

From a man in Phoenix, Arizona: "The sexual behavior material is bound to attract attention, particularly from deviates and those of the gray world, but is hardly suitable for inclusion in *The Independent* just because no one else will publish such tripe."

From a woman in Topeka, Kansas: "Discontinue my subscription. Your articles by Albert Ellis and other features are absolutely vile."

From a virgin in Lancaster, Pennsylvania: "That sex article (Adultery: Pros and Cons) is absolutely hideous. The writer of your article should be in jail. I wish to tell you I am a virgin. After my mother died, two men at different times wished to marry me. So don't get the idea I was forgotten. The decision to remain a virgin is my business.

"Furthermore, as pertains to that horrible sex article, I wish to tell you I believe in the King James version of the Bible from cover to cover. It says: You dare not commit fornication or adultery. God have mercy on Dr. Kinsey and the man who wrote your sex article. . . ."

And so on, and so forth. Considering that *The Independent* is decidedly a liberal paper, that it is sold mostly by subscription, and that its readers are generally well educated and enlightened, it is somewhat surprising that so much antisexual sentiment is provoked by my monthly column. Not that the anti-Ellis letters are necessarily typical of reader reaction: since, from long experience with publishing controversial material, I have found that people who oppose one's views are more likely to write excoriating letters to the editor, while people who approve are likely to write directly to the author or, more commonly, to keep their favorable opinions to themselves.

Nonetheless, I think it significant that so many of *The Independent's* readers, most of whom are probably men and women of good will with liberal attitudes on a host of politico-economic issues, become embarrassedly and angrily red-faced when confronted by reasonably liberal sex views. This is not the first time I have noticed that some of our most violent and virulent "radicals" are, at one and the same time, proper prudes.

The detractors of my *Independent* sex articles, however, have not entirely monopolized the field. My own files include a good many letters from favorable correspondents; and Lyle Stuart tells me that he meets many Ellis fans who never bother to write me or the

14

paper. Included in *The Independent*'s published letters on the Ellis controversy are these:

From a female psychology student: "The article on masturbation is worth the subscription price for a hundred years. It is so normal and natural an explanation."

From a man in Chicago: "Am very much pleased with the articles Dr. Albert Ellis has been presenting in your paper. I have long been impressed by the fact that he is one of the very few psychologists capable of being honest all the way with society."

From a correspondent in Whittier, California: "Ellis . . . is a man not afraid to tell the truth."

From a professional worker in Portland, Oregon: "I am still pro-Ellis. . . . May he keep up his good work of presenting the facts of life rather than the reflection of what the moralists think things should be."

From a man in Boulder, Colorado: "I especially appreciate the articles by Dr. Ellis, and that they are undoubtedly undeleted and unchanged from the way he submitted them."

From a correspondent in Ridgefield, New Jersey: "Here are four hearty cheers for your Albert Ellis articles!"

From a man in Cleveland, Ohio: "I am a pro-Ellis enthusiast, and I agree with Dr. Ellis whole-heartedly that when it comes to sexual hypocrisy, we Americans are its greatest champions."

Evidently, from the tone of these letters, the lynch-Ellis coterie is not entirely in the saddle. Vociferous, yes; but not quite unanimous. And among the most loyal supporters of my right to print heretical sex views, if not always a supporter of these views themselves, has been Lyle Stuart, who reaffirmed his faith in this right in an editorial which appeared in *The Independent* at the time many cancellations were being received because of my columns on premarital sex relations. Said the editor:

"Dr. Albert Ellis writes about sex matters. Although he is prominent in his field, some of the things that he has written in some of the articles were not allowed to appear in books that he authored or in papers that he read before learned societies.

"Does that mean that we approve of everything Dr. Ellis writes? Not at all. It means that we approve of Dr. Ellis's saying what he wants to say, frankly and without censorship."

The controversy raged up to the time I wrote my final regular column for *The Independent* and flares up again whenever I write new pieces, as I now and then do, for this periodical. A woman in Sun Valley, California attacks: "I am increasingly ashamed to have your paper brought to my mailbox. I would not have believed it possible to publish such material as the Ellis articles in the United States." And a wife in Yoder, Wyoming replies: "We like *The Independent* as it is, including the articles by Dr. Ellis. Why don't those who object to them just ignore them? Can't resist them, I'll bet. And then they are so-o-o shocked!"

Meanwhile, the chief inciter of this storm continues

to go about his nefarious business, turning out pieces on sex, love, and marriage for one of the few periodicals in America that will uncensoringly print them. And continue along these same lines I shall, until I run out of words or *The Independent* out of ink. Although, at the present time, I am mainly engrossed in developing a new theory and technique of psychotherapy, which I call rational therapy, and shall therefore interrupt my sexual columnizing for awhile, I—and *The Independent*—shall probably be back.

Here, then, are the still unbowdlerized articles which appeared in my eventful two years as *The Independent's* columnist. Some of them, which were continued in two or three successive issues of the paper, have been consolidated into single chapters; and others have been somewhat augmented, because of the more liberal space allowances available between the covers of a book. In all essentials, however, these essays are identical with those appearing in Lyle Stuart's unique periodical. If this be sex heresy, please make the most of it.

ALBERT ELLIS

New York City

SEX WITHOUT GUILT

1.

New Light on Masturbation

Although attitudes toward masturbation have become enormously more liberal during the past decade or two, it is still rare for writers on sex to take a wholly unequivocal stand on autoerotism. The point is continually made that masturbation is not as bad as it was once said to be; but the concomitant point that it is actually good and beneficial is rarely stated.

Censorship of outspoken articles on the subject is especially rife: so much so in fact that the original version of this article was refused admittance in a book which I edited and a scientific journal of which I was associate editor; and when it was given as part of an important symposium on religion and sex, the entire symposium was never published.

At this same symposium, several prominent psychologists and psychiatrists objected strenuously to my statement that masturbation is quite harmless by pointing out that it is sometimes accompanied by neurotic or perverted fantasies. The fact that, quite frequently, heterosexual coitus is also accompanied by neurotic or perverted fantasies they did not, of course, stress.

Now that the first four comprehensive Kinsey volumes have appeared, together with relevant anthropological material by Clellan Ford and Frank Beach, historical and sociological information by Lester Dearborn, and psychoanalytic data by Rene Spitz and others, we might do well to take another look at the problem of autoerotism, to try to see it in a more objective light than that which is usually shed on it.

It should come as no surprise, of course, that Dr. Kinsey and his associates found that about 93 per cent of their male and 62 per cent of their female subjects masturbate at some time during their lives.

It is perhaps more significant, however, when they inform us that the female tends to reach orgasm more easily and quickly by masturbation than by any other sex technique; that masturbation is much the most important source of sexual outlet for the unmarried females studied; and that females who masturbate have

NEW LIGHT ON MASTURBATION

a considerably better chance of achieving orgasm after marriage than those who do not.

As any serious student of sex knows, it is virtually impossible for most human beings to suppress their biological impulses completely, and if these impulses do not show themselves through so-called "normal" manifestations, they will frequently take "abnormal" forms of outlet—including "perverted" and neurotic symptoms.

One would think, therefore, that a society such as our own, which forcefully opposes premarital and extramarital sex relations, would welcome masturbation as a convenient, discreet mode of sex activity which makes it possible for almost any human being, if he or she wishes, to have a satisfying orgasmic release if and when most other forms of outlet are barred. In this respect, our own society is thoroughly illogical. For not only does it ban all sex outlets except marital intercourse, but it also discourages masturbation.

Not that matters in this respect are as bad as they used to be. Not quite. But where old time sex books promulgated an honest puritanism that was forthrightly anti-masturbational, modern manuals are often subtly, and essentially more dishonestly, antisexual in this connection.

In a recent communication, for example, the staff of the Child Study Association of America, consisting largely of trained psychiatric social workers, tells us that certainly masturbation "does not lead to blindness, brain fever, impotence, or any other physical or sexual

23

ill-effects." This Child Study Association staff then goes on, however, to point out that because children in our culture do get the idea that masturbation is dangerous, and consequently become guilty about their autoerotism, "perhaps the best course is for parents reassuringly to ally themselves with the child's own conscience in this matter and while assuring him that the practice will not harm him, also help him to find ways to grow out of it."

A more pernicious attitude than this could hardly be found. Essentially, it is the old puritanical view on masturbation brought in again by the back door after it has ostensibly been kicked out the front.

Obviously, if children do get the idea that masturbation is dangerous, they get it from someone; and if this idea is a false one—as it most definitely is—it should be unceremoniously and solidly annihilated, instead of being cowardly accepted and perpetuated.

In non-sexual areas, no one, and certainly not a group of clinicians, would ever make an equivalent mistake. Many children believe, for example, that breaking a mirror, failing to knock on wood at certain times, or passing in front of a black cat is dangerous, and become anxious when they engage in such activities. Are we, then, to ally ourselves with these children's puerile, misled ideas and try to help them grow out of breaking mirrors or passing in front of black cats? Or are we not, rather, to show them how silly their fears are in these connections, and how effectively to overcome the *fears* instead of stopping the *actions* leading to the fears?

24

NEW LIGHT ON MASTURBATION

So with masturbation. Of course, in this inhibited antisexual culture, children feel that masturbation is dangerous and become guilty when they engage in it. All the more reason, then, to disabuse them of this childish fear, and to teach them to accept masturbation in its true light—as a thoroughly undangerous, beneficial human act.

Similarly with the other neopuritanical notions in regard to autoerotism which clutter our most modern sex education texts. Let us, once and for all, say the final scientific, clinically based nay to these anti-masturbational notions. Some of the main quibbles which may be demolished are the following:

1. *The objection that masturbation is immature.* Masturbation is not in the least an immature, adolescent sex act, but is just as mature as any other mode. As Kinsey shows, in unmarried college level males between the ages of 26 and 30, masturbation provides 46 per cent of their total sex outlet; and in women between 36 and 45 years of age, 54 per cent of the single, 36 per cent of the married, and 58 per cent of the previously married subjects admitted masturbating. In view of these facts, to call masturbation an immature or adolescent activity is completely to ignore the facts of human sexuality.

Autoerotism may be called abnormal or deviant when an individual who has the choice of several other outlets, such as heterosexual relations in addition to masturbation, finds that he or she can *only* experience masturbatory satisfaction. Such individuals exist but appear to be quite rare. Virtually all other individuals who masturbate, at whatever age, are in the normal sexual range.

2. *The objection that masturbation is unsocial.* The idea that masturbation is a lonely, unsocial habit that will lead men and women to avoid the company of others because they satisfy themselves sexually is thoroughly ridiculous. It makes as much sense as the notion that going to a movie is socially healthier than viewing television at home or that individuals who read at home are poor lonely souls while all socially healthy persons read in libraries.

A girl or fellow who is unsocial and who fears facing others may well masturbate instead of trying to achieve heterosexual relations; but rare indeed is the individual who becomes unsocial *because* of masturbation. About *guilt* over masturbation, yes; but not over masturbation itself.

The one mode of sex behavior which most encourages loneliness and isolation would appear to be complete sexual abstinence, including abstinence from masturbation. If moralists wish to minimize human loneliness and unsociability, let them try to do something about *that.*

3. *The objection that masturbation does not lead to full emotional gratification.* The idea that masturba-

tion is relatively condemnable because it is an act which is incapable of giving individuals full emotional gratification is a notion that is, at best, partly true. In the first place, many people, particularly those with good fantasizing powers, do obtain what to them is a fair measure of emotional gratification from masturbating.

Secondly, no sex act—including heterosexual coitus —can, nor for that matter necessarily should, give full emotional gratification at all times to all persons. The concept that every sex act, in order to be considered a "good" and "beneficial" one, must be intensely emotionally satisfying, or that sex without love is wickedness, is a non-scientific, basically puritanical notion.

The Kinsey report on women shows that, unlike men, women do not necessarily need intense psychological or emotional accompaniments to their sex participations. What they often need, to achieve fully satisfying orgasms, is not romantic and emotional stimuli—which may actually distract them from sex concentration—but consistent, correctly applied friction and pressure to the most sensitive parts of their genitals.

It may well be, therefore, that much of the romanticism and emotionalism which women are *supposed* to need for sex satisfaction is largely the invention of the psychologically differently acclimated male, and that romantic love is often a saboteur, rather than an encourager, of female orgasm. In any event, the idea that masturbation is not emotionally gratifying and that it

27

therefore cannot be too satisfactory a sex procedure is, at best, only partially true, and tends to be greatly exaggerated by antisexual writers.

4. *The objection that masturbation is sexually frustrating.* Although masturbation, for most persons, is not as sexually satisfying as, say, coitus, it is by no means always frustrating. When it is frustrating or emotionally unsatisfying, it has often been *made* so because individuals in our culture are raised to *believe* that it should be so.

A man or woman who has been reared with violently anti-masturbational attitudes will naturally find autoerotism relatively unsatisfactory. One who has been raised with pro-masturbational attitudes will normally find it quite sexually satisfying—though not, usually, as much so as various forms of interhuman contact (H. Ellis, 1936).

5. *The objection that masturbation leads to impotence or frigidity.* Although it has frequently been held that autoerotism leads to impotence or premature ejaculation in males, there is no objective data to support this belief.

The notion that female masturbation conditions women so that they cannot enjoy coital satisfaction is completely contradicted by the Kinsey researchers, who find that among the females studied who never masturbated to orgasm before marriage, 31 to 37 per cent failed to reach coital orgasm during the early years of their marriage, while among those who had masturbated before marriage, only 13 to 16 per cent were coitally unresponsive in the early years of marriage. My own clinical studies, over a period of many years, also conclusively show that many women are definitely helped to achieve satisfactory marital relations if they first engage in some amount of masturbatory activity.

6. *The objection that masturbation may lead to sexual excess.* The idea that masturbation is likely to be taken to excess is another myth of neopuritanical origin. As has been noted for many years in the sexological literature, and as Kinsey has recently confirmed, erotic response, in both males and females, depends upon a remarkably foolproof mechanism. When an individual reaches the limits of his or her physiologic endurance, he or she no longer responds erotically. The male becomes totally incapacitated at this point, in that he is incapable of having further erections; and the female is able to have intercourse, but is neither benefited nor harmed by it.

Under the circumstances, only a most abnormal individual, such as a psychotic, would masturbate when he or she had no desire, and might consequently do so to "excess." The idea of a normal individual's actually engaging in "excessive" masturbation is ludicrous.

Altogether, then, the weasel-worded attitudes on masturbation which still fill most of our sex manuals, attitudes which state or imply that autoerotism, while

29

not completely harmful, is still not "good" or "desirable," have no scientific foundation and constitute a modern carryover of old antisexual moralizings.

The fact is that the vast majority of American males and females engage in a considerable amount of masturbation for some period during their lives; and that, particularly in view of our other restrictions on sexual activity, they would be most abnormal if they did not.

It is difficult to conceive of a more beneficial, harmless, tension-releasing human act than masturbation that is spontaneously performed without (puritanically-inculcated and actually groundless) fears and anxieties. Let us, please, now that Clark (1958), Dearborn (1961), Kinsey et al. (1948, 1953), the Kronhausens (1964), Mead (1939), Spitz (1949), Stekel (1950), and other modern authorities have stoutly reaffirmed this fact, see that our sex manuals and sex education texts unequivocally say it in plain English.

2.

Thoughts on Petting

Like masturbatory activities, petting generally has a bad name in our society. It has been variously claimed, by authorities as well as laymen, that petting for its own sake or petting to the point of orgasm is abnormal, perverted, unhealthy, immature, frustrating, frigidicizing, etc. Is there any truth to these allegations? Virtually none.

Let us start our discussion of petting with a few essential definitions. By petting we usually mean sexual stimulation of another human being that is done for its own sake rather than as a prelude to intercourse. It may or may not culminate in orgasm for either or both of the partners engaging in petting. It largely consists of tactile contact with the partner's body, particularly with this partner's erogenous zones; and it is usually done through caressing, embracing, kissing, biting, massaging, etc. (Ellis, 1961a).

When confined to lip kissing and mild embracing, petting is sometimes called *necking*. When it includes mutual nudity or stimulation of the genitals, it is often called *heavy petting*.

There is considerable condemnation of petting in the sexological literature, but most of this applies only to prolonged petting that does not lead to orgasmic release. According to some authorities, such non-climax-producing petting may result, for some individuals, in states of tension, pains in the groin or testicular region, headaches, and other signs of physical discomfort (Leader, 1959).

It is also possible that pelvic congestion resulting from such prolonged petting without release may lead to ailments of the genital tract; or that general tension produced by this kind of petting may lead to conditions of bodily stress that ultimately result in ulcers, high blood pressure, or other stress-induced ailments. Clear-cut instances of such dire results of petting without climax are, however, rare, and if they occur at all probably only occur in individuals who are, for various other reasons, easily susceptible to psychosomatic ailments.

On the other hand, it would appear that literally millions of individuals, especially great numbers of females in our society, are able to engage in steady and prolonged petting sessions with little or no harm and with some amount of satisfaction and tension reduction. It would seem, with these individuals, that petting for its own sake is more fulfilling and beneficial than not engaging in any form of sex relations whatever. At the same time, it must be strongly suspected that most of these individuals would derive still greater fulfillment and benefit from petting to orgasm (Harper, 1961a).

Petting to climax, when it is not engaged in exclusively or compulsively, would appear to have no serious disadvantages when compared to participation in actual coitus. It is frequently not as pleasurable an activity as is coitus, particularly for the male; but, on the other hand, many people, especially females, find it distinctly more satisfying than intercourse.

Petting to climax involves, in all the major details, almost exactly the same kind of stimulation and response as does coitus. This is particularly true when it involves, as it easily may, intravaginal petting, with the male entering the female's vagina with his fingers instead of his penis. As far as can presently be determined, most men and women experience quite the same kind of orgasm through petting as they do through copulation —providing that they do not have some significant psychological prejudices in favor of one of these two kinds of sex acts (Masters and Johnson, 1961, 1962).

When it is practiced exclusively as a means of achieving orgasm, or is invariably preferred to all other forms

33

of sex relations, petting may be a form of sexual fetishism, compulsiveness, or neurosis. Thus, it may be exclusively resorted to as a means of sexual outlet because the individual is illogically afraid of having intercourse, or would be guilty about technical loss of virginity, or is fetishistically attached to some mode of sexuality, such as breast manipulation, which is part of petting procedures.

Exclusive resort to petting, then, may constitute a form of sexual deviation. But not necessarily! It is quite possible for a given person to prefer petting to orgasm to all other forms of sexual contact, and therefore invariably to engage in petting rather than, say, coitus and for this person to be unneurotic.

Take, by way of illustration, the case of a male who has a very sensitive meatus (opening of his urethral tract at the end of his penis) and who consequently finds it somewhat painful to engage in intercourse. As second choice, this male may virtually always prefer to pet to orgasm, and may be perfectly reasonable or sane in his preference.

Another male may find that he is so sexually sensitive that when he engages in copulation he has a climax quite quickly; while, when he has his wife caress his body or his sex organs lightly, he takes longer to come to climax and enjoys himself more thoroughly. Such an individual, again without being sexually deviant or neurotic, may invariably prefer petting to climax to intercourse.

By the same token, a female may find that intercourse is too stimulating to be highly enjoyable and may, instead, almost always want to achieve her orgasms through petting. Or, conversely, she may find (as women frequently find) that intercourse is too unstimulating to bring her to climax, while petting, particularly direct massage of her clitoris, is almost the only way in which she can readily obtain orgasm. Under such circumstances, a woman would hardly be abnormal or perverted if she exclusively preferred petting and only had intercourse from time to time for her husband's sake.

Petting to orgasm is particularly normal and healthy when it is resorted to because other forms of sex relations might result in real difficulties for the petters. Thus, if two young people, or even two older married people, want to have sex relations and want to make sure that they avoid pregnancy, they can safely obtain virtually all the satisfactions they want without having to take any risks. Or if two individuals can only have sex relations in a semi-public place—such as a parked automobile—and wish to minimize the danger of detection, petting may well be a more practicable form of sex involvement than coitus (Reevy, 1961).

It is most surprising—as Dr. Alex Comfort has pointed out in his book, *Sexual Behavior in Society*—that a culture such as our own, which frowns so heavily on premarital sex relations, and particularly stresses the dangers of illegitimate pregnancy and abortion, should also disapprove of petting to orgasm. For if young people tend to have strong sex desires—which they gen-

35

erally do—and if they are going to have some kind of sex participations—which they evidently are—it would seem far wiser to encourage them to pet to climax rather than, say, to have premarital coitus or to engage in homosexual activity.

Our own society, alas, is neither perceptive nor wise in this connection. It frowns upon premarital intercourse—as well as on the thoroughly undangerous sex acts, masturbation and petting. In so doing, it virtually ensures that there will be considerable copulation on the part of young people who, if they had been more rationally educated in sexual areas, would probably be petting to orgasm in most instances. A most peculiar paradox!

In any event, petting itself would seem to be relatively harmless for many individuals when it is carried on in its own right, and absolutely harmless when it is carried to the point of mutual orgasm. The vast majority of males and females can easily come to climax through various types of petting; and there seems to be no good reason why, when they want to, they should not.

3.

On Premarital Sex Relations

Many recent books on sex and marriage relations discuss the pros and cons of premarital intercourse, and virtually all of them wind up by being against it (Duvall, 1963; Mace, 1961; Sorokin, 1956).

Few of these texts, however, give an adequate discussion of the issue, since they list, with no grain of salt, many "disadvantages" of fornication which are more appropriate to the 1890's than today's America, while failing to list many advantages of premarital affairs.

SEX WITHOUT GUILT

A more sophisticated and fairer presentation of the pros and cons of sex before marriage rarely gets printed in these United States; and when it does, it certainly doesn't get widely circulated in school and college courses on sexuo-amative etiquette. Yet, all the facts at our disposal show that premarital relations have been unusually widespread for the last half century (Chesser, 1956; Ellis, 1965a; Ehrmann, 1960; Kirkendall, 1961; the Kronhausens, 1960; Reiss, 1960; Brown, 1964).

Just for the record, it might prove interesting to make a fairly complete list of the advantages and disadvantages of sex participation among the great American unwed. First, let us list, and with some degree of critical judgment appraise, the alleged evils of premarital copulation.

1. *The dangers of venereal disease.* Although uninformed and unintelligent people still are fairly frequent victims of VD, the infection rate among well-educated individuals is quite low. With the proper use of prophylactic devices, on the one hand, and modern antibiotics on the other, the informed person who engages in premarital sex activity today has small chance of suffering severely from a venereal infection.

2. *Illegitimate pregnancy and abortion.* Modern methods of birth control have been so well perfected today and seem to be much on the verge of even far greater effectiveness that so-called illegitimate pregnancy and abortion are rare among those who care-

38

fully and consistently employ the already existing techniques (Beigel, 1961, 1962).

3. *Guilt and anxiety*. Since premarital sex relations are no longer viewed as morally reprehensible or sinful by most educated and informed individuals, there need be no intrinsic guilt attached to them.

People who are anxious and guilty because of their premarital affairs are usually emotionally disturbed individuals who are also anxious and guilty about many of their non-sexual participations. On the other hand, many people today are becoming anxious and disturbed because they are *not* copulating before marriage.

4. *Loss of reputation*. Today's young people, including the young girls, are rarely severely condemned or ostracized for their premarital adventures. On the contrary, they are just as likely to lose the esteem of their fellows for remaining virginal as for being unchaste. People who mortally fear any loss of reputation because of their premarital proclivities are usually disturbed and need psychological treatment (Ellis, 1957, 1962a; Ellis and Harper, 1961a, 1961b).

5. *Frigidity or impotence*. While it used to be feared that individuals having premarital affairs would tend to become frigid or impotent in their later life, all reliable existing data (especially the Kinsey studies) tend to show the opposite. The more premarital sex activity a young person has, the more is he or she likely to

be sexually competent in his or her later life, including married life.

6. *Emotional risks.* Although it is quite true that those who engage in premarital affairs take risks, in the sense that these affairs may break up and they may thereby be hurt, it is also true that young people who love each other *without* sexual involvement take similar risks, and may just as easily be hurt. Besides, taking risks, and being disappointed in some of the things one does, are hardly necessarily harmful to a human being, but are part of the process of emotional growth and development. Youngsters who take *no* emotional risks are much more likely to become seriously aberrated.

7. *Exploitation of one's sex partner.* Exploitation of one's sex partner generally takes place when one individual (usually the male) has sex relations with another under false pretenses—pretending that he loves her, will marry her, or something on that order. Such exploitation doubtless often occurs in premarital affairs: not because of the affairs themselves, but because of the dishonesty of the people engaging in them.

Where both partners, moreover, frankly have sex relations for the sexual (as well as other) satisfactions they thereby derive, such exploitation is reduced to a minimum. Consequently, the more open, honest, and frequent premarital intercourse tends to become, the less does it remain potentially exploitative.

8. *Sabotage of family life.* It has often been alleged that premarital sex relations sabotage family life and keep people from marrying and raising good families. There seems to be no scientific evidence to support this belief, and much contrary evidence which tends to show that individuals who have premarital sex experience marry more easily, and are more relaxed about raising their children (especially about educating their children sexually) than those who rigorously abstain.

If premarital affairs really destroyed family life, the human race would have long since died out: since young men of virtually all times and places have usually liberally engaged in such affairs (Ford and Beach, 1962; Taylor, 1962; Waldemar, 1960).

9. *Sex without love.* Premarital copulation, it is alleged, leads to sex without love. This is sheer nonsense: since most of the great love affairs of human history, such as that of Heloise and Abelard, appear to have consisted of fornicative ones. Sex, no matter how it is indulged, normally creates and enhances love (Hunt, 1962).

Virginity, especially when it is prolonged and taken to extremes, seems to be the true enemy of love (and often engenders deep-seated hostility to others). Sex without love, moreover, is hardly a heinous crime, and appears to be quite delightful and to add immeasurably to the lives of literally millions of individuals (Ellis, 1963a, 1963b).

10. *Sordid surroundings.* Premarital intercourse, it is said, is often performed hastily, in sordid surroundings, under the fear of discovery and other poor conditions. Perhaps this was so in the nineteenth century; but the vast majority of today's premarital acts are performed in places and under conditions which are often just as good (and far more romantic and exciting) than those existing during marital relations. And they are arranged so that fear of discovery (or any great to-do about actual discovery) is minimal.

11. *Lack of respect for partner's conviction.* It is contended that those who have fornicative relations often do not respect their partners' convictions against such relations. This is the veriest drivel: since very few persons, in our society, *force* or *coerce* another to have intercourse with them.

One partner may well talk the other partner out of his or her prior convictions against sex activity; but surely this is just as legitimate in sex as in politics, religion, or any other field where people have convictions.

12. *Lack of responsibility.* It is often objected that those who fornicate obtain all the pleasures of sex without any of the responsibilities of marriage. But why, if that is what they want, shouldn't they? Couples who date platonically, or love each other without sex relations, or who play tennis together also obtain satisfactions without assuming any of the responsibilities of marriage.

Why *must* everyone marry to be a good citizen?

And, even assuming that most people will eventually marry—which, statistically speaking, is a fact-based assumption—why should they marry and assume responsibilities with *every* person they are sexually attracted toward, fall in love with, or want to have as a tennis partner?

13. *Subsequent adultery.* It is said that those who have premarital affairs are more likely to engage in adultery after marriage. Granted that this may be so (for there is at least a little factual evidence that would seem to point in this direction), it has never been shown that those who copulate premaritally engage in considerable adultery after marriage, nor that they were adulterous because of their premarital affairs, nor that their adultery is particularly inimical to their marriages.

On the contrary, there is some evidence that adultery may aid, save, and stabilize a marriage rather than disrupt it and lead to its dissolution.

14. *Suspicion of adultery.* It is contended that if an individual has premarital sex relations with his (or her) mate he will then keep suspecting that he (or she) may, after marriage, have adulterous affairs with others.

This is simply not true: for the vast majority of those who have premarital sex relations (which means the majority of people now marrying in America) definitely do not keep suspecting their mates of adultery—

except, of course, where they have some cause to do so.

Anyone who would suspect his mate of being adulterous merely because she had premarital sex relations would be quite insecure and disturbed himself, and in definite need of psychological help.

15. *Lack of happiness in marriage.* It has been reported in several studies that individuals who have premarital sex relations, especially promiscuous ones, are less happily married than those who are virginal at marriage. This finding is exceptionally dubious, in that individuals who are afraid and ashamed to have premarital affairs are precisely the same kind of individuals who would be afraid and ashamed to admit, even to themselves, that their marriages are unhappy.

Clinical evidence would tend to show just the contrary: namely, that people today who have premarital sex relations are generally happier in marriage than those who do not.

16. *Promiscuity.* It is often held that if an individual has premarital sex relations he or she will become promiscuous. This is simply not true: since the vast majority of men and, especially, women who have had antenuptial affairs have had them with relatively few individuals and have been very far from promiscuous.

Indeed, exceptionally few people in our society are ever really promiscuous—since promiscuity means indiscriminateness in one's choice of sex partners, and it is

44

the rare person who is really indiscriminate in this regard.

When promiscuity does exist it may be a symptom of (a) unusually high sex desires and capacities or (b) emotional disturbance. These symptoms are hardly likely to *result from* premarital sex relations but often may be a *cause* of such relations.

17. *Unachievable ideal.* It is sometimes held that premarital sex relations are often so satisfying and premarital affairs so free and adventurous, that marriage suffers by comparison and cannot easily compete with this lovely ideal. This may sometimes be true. But if people did not have premarital affairs, the relationships that they would consequently *imagine,* would be even more glamorous and adventurous than marriage and would serve as unfair comparison to it.

Many individuals can only tolerate marriage because they have, in practice, seen the disadvantages as well as the advantages of having affairs before marriage. The more such affairs they have, the more realistic they tend to be, and the more likely they are to accept the limitations of marriage.

The foregoing alleged limitations and horrors of premarital intercourse are not exhaustive, but would appear to give an adequate coverage of the main points that are commonly raised in this connection. As can be seen by the chief rebuttals presented, virtually all these objections to antenuptial affairs never had too much validity in the first place or, if they were once valid, applied largely to conditions existing many decades ago.

Today, the same objections are largely captious and specious as far as the average intelligent informed individual who is having premarital affairs is concerned. They may well apply to the ignorant, the stupid, and the seriously disturbed; but not notably to the well-informed, bright, and reasonably well-adjusted young people of our society.

The other side of the story—the advantages of premarital affairs—will now be briefly outlined. This is the side which is especially conspicuously absent from virtually all published writings on the subject.

There are, nonetheless, many obvious benefits to be derived from antenuptial sex relations. Here are some of them:

1. *Sexual release.* Most human beings require some form of steady sexual release for their maximum healthfulness, happiness, and efficient functioning. If these individuals are not married—which many millions of them, of course, are not—perhaps the best form of relief from sexual tension they may obtain is through having heterosexual premarital relations.

2. *Psychological release.* In many, though by no means all instances, individuals who do not have premarital affairs are beset with serious psychosexual strain and conflict and tend to be obsessed with sexual thoughts and feelings. Most of these individuals can be

considerably relieved of their psychosexual hypertension if they have satisfactory nonmarital affairs.

3. *Sexual competence.* In sexual areas, as in most other fields of human endeavor, practice makes perfect and familiarity breeds contempt for fear. In the cases of millions of unmarried males and females who are relatively impotent or frigid, there is little doubt that if they engaged in steady heterosexual relations they would become enormously more sexually competent.

4. *Ego enhancement.* Although, as noted in the first section of this chapter, engaging in premarital affairs involves distinct risks, especially the risks of being rejected or emotionally hurt, there is almost no other way that a human being can enhance his self-esteem and desensitize himself to emotional vulnerability except by deliberately taking such risks.

Confirmed male and female virgins in our culture usually dislike themselves immensely, knowing that they do not have the guts to live.

5. *Adventure and experience.* A rigorous restraint from premarital affairs leads to neutrality or nothingness: to a lack of adventure and experience. Particularly in this day and age, when there are few remaining frontiers to explore and unscaled mountains to climb, nonmarital affairs furnish a prime source of sensory-esthetic-emotional experimentation and learning.

SEX WITHOUT GUILT

6. *Improved marital selection.* Because marriage, in our society, is usually infrequent and long-lasting for any given individual, the person who marries should have the kind of knowledge and training that will best fit him to make a good marital choice. There is little doubt that the very best experience he can acquire in this connection is to have one or more premarital affairs and, through these affairs, be able to discover much relevant information about himself and members of the other sex.

Moreover: the individual who has such affairs is well able to wait patiently until he is in a good psychological and socio-economic condition to marry; while he who has no such affairs is often impelled to make a rash and poorly selected marriage out of (conscious or unconscious) sexual deprivation (Brown, 1962).

7. *Prophylaxis against sexual deviation.* As will be pointed out elsewhere in this book, many individuals in our society become involved in fixed or exclusive homosexuality, or in other forms of sex fetishism or perversion, largely because they do not have ample opportunity for early heterosexual involvements. Premarital relations doubtless constitute the best possible prophylaxis to the development of serious psychosexual deviations.

8. *Heterosexual democratization.* The maintenance of premarital virginity, particularly among females, almost inevitably leads to a double standard of sex

48

morality and to fascistic-type discrimination against equal rights for women. Widespread premarital affairs invariably break down this autocratic, anti-female attitude and lead to real democracy and equality between the sexes.

9. *Decrease in jealousy.* Violent jealousy between men and women is largely the result of the banning of extramarital affairs and the viewing of one's mate as one's exclusive property. This kind of pathological jealousy would probably tend to be distinctly reduced if a more liberal attitude toward premarital affairs were extant.

10. *De-emphasis on pornography.* The increasing emphasis on the female form and on pornographic presentations that is currently so widespread in our culture is largely fomented by our restrictions on premarital sexuality. The more an individual engages in satisfactory and consistent premarital relations, the less he will usually be inclined to be interested in second-hand picturizations of sex (Ellis, 1962b; Ellis, 1963c).

11. *Savings in time and energy.* Considerable time is wasted in our society by individuals constantly *seeking* for direct or indirect sex gratifications in the path of which we place unusual obstacles. Those persons who actually engage in steady premarital affairs save this kind of wasted effort and at least considerably *enjoy* the time that they do devote to sexual participations.

49

12. *Ending of sex discrimination.* Many individuals in our culture for one reason or another do not care to marry or are in no position to do so for the present. There is no reason why these individuals should be discriminated against *sexually* merely because they are nonmaritally inclined.

By permitting these individuals to have premarital affairs, antisexual discriminations against them would thereby be removed. As things stand, however, many such individuals, who really should not marry or procreate, are literally driven into unhappy matings because they require sex outlets.

13. *Sexual varietism.* Many individuals have distinct needs for sexual varietism, especially during certain periods of their lives. The most practical way for these persons to fulfill their needs is through premarital affairs.

14. *Limiting prostitution.* There is no question that wherever premarital sex relations on a voluntary basis become more common, prostitutional relations tend to decrease considerably. If prostitution is thought to have distinct dangers and hazards, then the best way to eradicate these would be to encourage premarital non-prostitutional affairs.

15. *Limiting abortion, illegitimacy, and veneral disease.* If the facts of premarital relations were squarely faced and provided for, it would be a relatively simple

matter to minimize or eradicate the danger of abortion, illegitimacy, and venereal disease. It is by combatting premarital affairs that we fruitlessly employ efforts that could much better be spent in eliminating certain dangers which, almost entirely because of puritan bolstering, are still connected with such affairs.

16. *Inhibiting sex offenses.* Most sex offenders, as demonstrated in the book, *The Psychology of Sex Offenders* (Ellis and Brancale, 1956), are not overly impulsive, promiscuous individuals with wide-spread experience; on the contrary, they are overly-inhibited, constricted persons with relatively little heterosexual experience. If these individuals would engage in more frequent, more satisfying premarital affairs, there is little doubt that many of them would commit fewer sex offenses.

17. *Sex is fun.* As has been previously noted by myself and others, sex is fun; heterosexual relations, in particular, are the very best fun; and more heterosexual relations are still more fun.

Assuming that human beings who remain virginal till marriage are more pure and saintly than those who do not, the thesis cannot very well be upheld that they are commonly happier and more joyful. To fornicate may be "sinful"; but it is also a rare delight. Perhaps we would be saner to work at making it less rare rather than less delightful (Benjamin and Masters, 1964; Guyon, 1961; Stokes, 1962).

51

This, then, is a nonexhaustive list of some of the main advantages of premarital sex relations. Such a list does not indicate, of course, that antenuptial intercourse is good for all persons at all times under all circumstances. Obviously, it is not.

Many unwed individuals, for instance, may prefer not to engage in coitus simply because the risks of pregnancy, however slight when proper precautions are taken, still do exist. Others may decide to refrain from heavy petting with certain members of the other sex, because they would then tend to become too emotionally involved with these individuals, and prefer not to be so involved.

There are certainly good reasons, then, why, in some instances, some persons may prefer to be celibate, or may only engage in petting rather than coitus. The relevant question, however, is not: *Must* a healthy young person engage in premarital affairs? It is rather: *May* an informed and intelligent individual in our culture justifiably and guiltlessly have coitus before marriage?

On the basis of the existing evidence, viewed quite apart from the myths which are so widely published and broadcast in this area, it is exceptionally difficult to see why he or she may not.

1.

Adultery: Pros and Cons

We have now considered the pros and cons of pre-marital sex relations and come to the conclusion that it is exceptionally difficult to see why well-informed, bright, and reasonably well-adjusted young people in our society may not justifiably engage in antenuptial affairs.

The question now before us is: Should the same conclusion be reached about adultery? More specifically: Granted that, for a variety of reasons, adultery was a hazardous venture in preceding centuries, and that the

Sixth Commandment *once* made sound sense, is the case against extramarital relations still valid *today?*

Let us admit, at the outset, that many of the old grounds for opposing adultery are just as senseless, in today's world, as many similar grounds for combatting premarital sex affairs. For example:

Intelligent and informed modern men and women do not consider adultery intrinsically wicked and sinful and therefore often commit it with little or no guilt or anxiety.

They are well able, with use of up-to-date contraceptive techniques, to avoid the dangers of illegitimate pregnancy and abortion; and with the employment of prophylactic measures and the selection of appropriate partners, they can easily avoid venereal infection.

They often need not worry about loss of reputation, since in many segments of modern society they are likely to gain rather than lose reputation by engaging in extramarital affairs.

They need not commit adultery under sordid conditions, or on a non-loving basis, as they frequently can arrange to have highly amative and affectional, and sometimes exceptionally rewarding, affairs.

They need not jeopardize their marriages, because as the Kinsey research group has shown, adulterous affairs which are not known to one's mate can actually help enhance and preserve one's marriage rather than serve to sabotage or destroy it.

In view of these facts of modern life, it is most doubtful whether many of the old telling arguments against adultery still hold too much water. At the same time, several of the indubitable advantages of premarital sex relations, which we examined in the previous chapter, also hold true for adultery.

Thus, it may be said with little fear of scientific contradiction, that literally millions of men and women who engage in adulterous affairs thereby gain considerable adventure and experience, become more competent at sexual pursuits and practices, are enabled to partake of a high degree of varietism, and have substantial amounts of sexual and nonsexual fun that they otherwise would doubtlessly be denied. These, in a world that tends to be as dull and drab for the average man as our own, are no small advantages.

Should, then, the informed and intelligent husband and wife in our society blithely go about committing adultery? The answer, paradoxically enough, seems to be, in most cases, no. Why so? For several reasons:

1. Although, in some ideal society, it is quite probable that husbands and wives could be adulterous with impunity, and might well gain more than lose thereby, ours is definitely not such an ideal society. For better or worse, we raise individuals to *feel* that their marriages are in jeopardy and that they are unloved if their mates have extramarital affairs.

Whether, under these circumstances, adultery actually *does* destroy marriages or *does* prove lack of love, is beside the point. Once one is raised to *feel* that these things are true, they tend to *become* true; and, under adulterous circumstances, damage often *is* therefore done to marriage. It would probably be much better if intelligent spouses convinced themselves that they *could* continue to love each other and live amicably together while still, at least occasionally, permitting themselves above-board extramarital affairs; but when they do not adopt this kind of sensible attitude toward adultery, they definitely endanger their marriages by engaging in it.

2. Because people in our culture *believe* adultery to be inimical to marriage, husbands and wives who engage in extramarital relations generally have to do so secretly and furtively. This means that they must be dishonest with their mates; and, although their adultery, in itself, might not harm their marriages, their *dishonesty* about this adultery (as about any other major issue) may well prove to be harmful.

3. Because, in our society, married couples are supposed to achieve sex satisfaction only with each other, if one mate is an adulterer he will often tend to have less sex interest in the other mate than he normally would have; and, in consequence, she may very well become sexually deprived and maritally discontent.

4. By the same token, since most individuals in our society are limited as to their financial resources, time, energy, etc., an adulterous mate by devoting efforts to his (or her) inamorata may well deprive his mate in these non-sexual respects.

5. If an individual has a good all-around marriage, in terms of the satisfaction of his love, sex, companion-

ship, familial, and other desires; and if his mate might well be quite unhappy and might possibly divorce him if he were discovered to be engaging in an adulterous affair; he would then be jeopardizing his marriage for additional satisfactions which might hardly be worth the risk.

Under these circumstances, an individual who has a good or an excellent marriage may be foolish to risk the breakup of this relationship largely for the opportunity of having additional sex pleasures—which are often likely to be his main gain from adultery. On the other hand, individuals who have poor marriages take no such risks, and often might just as well be caught in adulterous affairs.

6. In general, the risks one takes in committing adultery behind one's mate's back are the same risks one takes in making any major move behind her back. Thus, if one invests the family savings in a new Cadillac, or accepts a job in Alaska, or decides to discontinue the use of contraceptives without informing one's mate, one is hardly being maritally cooperative, and risks his or her severe displeasure.

By the same token, if one is secretly adulterous, one is usually not being too cooperative with one's mate, and therefore risks her eventually discovering this fact and being highly displeased (not to mention hysterical) because of it. Quite aside, then, from the sexual aspects of adultery, which are highly emphasized and exaggerated in our particular society, the secret commission of any major act with which one's mate is concerned is bound to affect one's relationship with this mate, and usually to affect it adversely.

This, then, would seem to be the major issue here: not adultery itself and its so-called moral consequences, but the consequences of being dishonest with one's mate, and through this dishonesty risking an impedance or destruction of mutual trust, confidence, and working partnership.

In view of these facts, it is questionable whether a well-adjusted, rational individual in our society should normally commit furtive adultery—at least, if he wants to perpetuate a presumably good marriage. If he is not himself married (but is committing adultery through having sex relations with someone who is), or if he is already unhappily married, then he may have nothing to lose by engaging in extramarital affairs.

If he is married happily enough, and he and his wife honestly and mutually believe that adultery is a good thing, and are not at all disturbed by the knowledge of each other's infidelities, then again he may have nothing to lose. But the chances of his and his mate's having such a liberal attitude toward adultery if they were both raised in our culture are (unfortunately!) slim.

Otherwise stated: It does not appear to be very difficult for intelligent and informed men and women in our civilization to accept fully the fact that premarital sex relations are a good thing and to become entirely guilt-free in this connection. But, as yet, it does appear to be most difficult for them to accept the fact that they and their mates may be adulterous without sabotaging their marriages. Several past and present societies other than our own have condoned adultery; and it is possible that we, too, may do so sometime in the future. For the present, however, adultery, except under certain limited circumstances (such as an individual's being away from home for a long time), would appear to be impractical rather than sinful for most people (Harper 1961b; Tatum, 1964).

Today's adulterer need not feel evil or wicked. But, from the standpoint of impairing his own marriage, he may well be acting irrationally and neurotically. If he thinks of adultery not in terms of sin but in terms of the possible *adulteration* of his own marital happiness, he should be able to make wiser choices in this connection.

After publishing the foregoing remarks in *The Independent,* I received a remarkable letter from a middle aged psychologist which raises some interesting questions in relation to adultery. My psychological correspondent, whom I shall call Dr. X, states that he married a childhood sweetheart when he was 25, had a so-so marriage with her, managed to have satisfactory sex relations, and was a faithful, most respectable husband and father (of five children) for 22 years. Finally, in his late forties, he had his first extramarital affair with "a handsome and attractive woman with a divine bell-like voice."

About this affair, Dr. X writes: "For the first time I was in love, and even more, for the first time I learned what passion could be. Very early I became sure it could not last—I was scared of my own inadequacy to keep pace with my lover's passion and with her genuine acceptance of what could be called free love.

"I was still pretty fiercely monogamous, though to my surprise I found no difficulty in having sexual relations with my lover and two days later, with my wife at home. My family obligations also kept me from even considering a divorce at this time."

Dr. X. insists that this relationship "did tremendous things for me" and even made his marriage better for a while.

A year later, after the first affair had ended, he contracted a love affair with the widow of a cherished friend while he was away from home for six months. He says that "nothing in the whole affair is remembered with regret—just steady, warm satisfaction. There was sorrow but no hurt in the parting. And as before, the effect on my marriage was to make me for a time more affectionate, more understanding of my wife, better able to put up with the difficulties of our basic incompatibility."

Dr. X then had an unsatisfactory affair with a woman much younger than he; and notes that "this relation did *not* help my marriage. Curious, isn't it? that when I find satisfaction elsewhere, my relation to my wife improves; when I fail elsewhere, it does not."

When his youngest child finished school, Dr. X received a divorce from his wife and later married a woman with whom he had for some time been having an adulterous affair. Both this woman and her former husband had been having, by mutual agreement, extra-marital affairs since the first year of their marriage. As long as they felt that their own marriage was solid they did not mind each other's infidelities.

On one occasion, the second Mrs. X and her first husband swapped partners with a couple with whom they were friendly, and all four lived amicably together under the same roof for several months. Finally, however, Mrs. X's first husband permanently took up with still another woman; and Dr. X's adulterous affair with her began, and later led to their marrying.

At this time, Dr. X reports, "I was still a bit more inclined to the monogamous point of view. She insisted that a nonrestricting attitude was a necessity for love, that one could not fully love while denying what might be a rewarding experience for the partner. I know that I grew in my understanding not of sex but of love, as we worked our way through this problem. I'd have given anything to have got some part of these insights before my earlier marriage.

"But I still wasn't sure. So one day, learning that my wife's first love, Carl, was passing through our city, suggested that she invite him to stop over for a visit. I deliberately courted the trial. Could I take it if she were to renew her old and sweet intimacy?

"I slept with her the night before Carl was to make an early arrival; then, before dawn, went away to give him a clear field. And I did find it in me to say to myself and deeply to feel: 'I want my darling to be happy with

Carl whatever form that happiness takes.' I think I really wanted them to have sex intimacy. At any rate, I went home full of a kind of pride in myself and a joyful loving peace. That was a high point in my whole life.

"Later, I joined Carl and my beloved for breakfast, and we had a fine time till his train arrived. It would be good to be able to say that I don't know nor care whether they had been intimate. I didn't ask but was told: she felt that our own relation was still too absorbing and rejected Carl's gentle inquiry. So in perfect honesty I said, 'Perhaps later you may feel otherwise. You know that if you do, I shall not be concerned.' Nor shall I."

Later, with another old lover of his wife's Dr. X's newly gained attitude was actually tested. Mrs. X comforted and slept with this old lover and told Dr. X what she had done. He notes: "I can say quite certainly that I was *glad* for her, and felt no loss of anything."

Dr. X concludes his letter with these observations: "Love is not a quantum that is lessened when divided. It is a growing system that increases with activity, like a living organism. True, it is subject, to use Gardner Murphy's term, to some degree of canalization. Constant adultering might divert love away from one person.

"In any kind of social arrangement there are grave problems regarding the management of love and sex. In our own society, adultery no doubt takes more intelligent thoughtfulness than is usually available. But I think we ought to keep in mind the *values* of multiple sex and love relations. Not just sex satisfaction alone, but love.

"That makes adultery dangerous. But it can mean great personal growth. I could not possibly love my wife as I do if it had not been for my adulterous love affairs. And she would not have been my beloved if she had not been able to open her love as she did to several men."

Dr. X's letter—the whole of which is ten pages long and has other pertinent things to say besides those quoted here—is most sincere and persuasive. In considering stories like his, and many more I have heard which are similar, I am compelled, once again, to be skeptical of all sweeping generalizations about human conduct.

Granted that a tabued and legally penalized mode of behavior, such as adultery, has its distinct disadvantages, it must also be admitted that it has real advantages.

Granted that it is silly, childish, and self-defeating under one set of circumstances, it can also be inordinately valuable and ennobling under other circumstances.

Granted that certain individuals in our anti-adulterous communities could never tolerate their own or their partners' extramarital affairs, it is clear that certain other individuals—such as Dr. and Mrs. X—can not only stoically bear, but actually find genuine satisfaction, in their own cuckoldry.

If we wish to be psychologically smug here, we may

insist that people like Dr. and Mrs. X, who are originally raised with the prevalent puritanical notions of our society, cannot possibly *really* accept their own or their spouses' adulterous affairs. We may say that, unconsciously if not consciously, their liberal and permissive attitudes toward sex are underlain by more resentful and guilty attitudes, and that therefore they cannot receive *genuine* happiness from accepting or engaging in adultery.

This kind of psychological analysis, however, borders on the unscientific, since it gets you going and coming. If you say that you like white, it insists that you really unconsciously prefer black but are afraid to admit this. And if you say that you like black, it says that you really, unconsciously prefer white. It leaves, this kind of "thinking," no room for *conscious* preferences.

Moreover, it is unconstructive and defeatist in that it denies all possibilities of basic human change. Admitting that human beings, once they have learned that white is good and black is bad, *have difficulty* in convincing themselves otherwise, this is not to say that they find changing their convictions *impossible.* If this were true, virtually no human progress would ever occur.

It is my firm conviction, therefore, that Dr. X *has,* in spite of his original puritanical upbringing, significantly changed his attitudes toward adultery, and that he *is* now able not merely resentfully to tolerate but actually to enjoy some of his wife's infidelities. And not, I would be willing to wager, because he is masochistic, repressive, or perverse—but because he is now more civilized, humane, and loving.

So much for Dr. X. The rest of us are actually the heart of the matter. Are *we* able to be happier, emotionally healthier, and more loving by being adulterous? In the main, considering what our (horrible) upbringing has been, I am afraid not. But even this is not the full answer.

The full answer, I think, is: Some of us are able to benefit from adultery and some of us are not. Do we dare, then, make an invariant rule for all?

5.

The Justification of Sex Without Love

A scientific colleague of mine, who holds a professorial post in the department of sociology and anthropology at one of our leading universities, recently asked me about my stand on the question of human beings having sex relations without love. Although I have taken something of a position on this issue in my book, *The American Sexual Tragedy*, I have never quite considered the problem in sufficient detail. So here goes.

In general, I feel that affectional, as against nonaffectional, sex relations are *desirable* but not *necessary*.

THE JUSTIFICATION OF SEX WITHOUT LOVE

It is usually desirable that an association between coitus and affection exist—particularly in marriage, because it is often difficult for two individuals to keep finely tuned to each other over a period of years, and if there is not a good deal of love between them, one may tend to feel sexually imposed upon by the other.

The fact, however, that the co-existence of sex and love may be desirable does not, to my mind, make it necessary. My reasons for this view are several:

1. Many individuals—including, even, many married couples—*do* find great satisfaction in having sex relations without love. I do not consider it fair to label these individuals as criminal just because they may be in the minority.

Moreover, even if they are in the minority (as may well *not* be the case), I am sure that they number literally millions of men and women. If so, they constitute a sizable subgroup of humans whose rights to sex satisfaction should be fully acknowledged and protected.

2. Even if we consider the supposed majority of individuals who find greater satisfaction in sex-love than in sex-sans-love relations, it is doubtful if all or most of them do so for *all* their lives. During much of their existence, especially their younger years, these people tend to find sex-without-love quite satisfying, and even to prefer it to affectional sex.

When they become older, and their sex drives tend to wane, they may well emphasize coitus with rather than without affection. But why should we condemn them *while* they still prefer sex to sex-love affairs?

3. Many individuals, especially females in our culture, who say that they only enjoy sex when it is accompanied by affection are actually being unthinkingly conformist and unconsciously hypocritical. If they were able to contemplate themselves objectively, and had the courage of their inner convictions, they would find sex without love eminently gratifying.

This is not to say that they would *only* enjoy non-affectional coitus, nor that they would always find it *more* satisfying than affectional sex. But, in the depths of their psyche and soma, they would deem sex without love pleasurable *too*.

And why should they not? And why should we, by our puritanical know-nothingness, force these individuals to drive a considerable portion of their sex feelings and potential satisfactions underground?

If, in other words, we view sexuo-amative relations as desirable rather than necessary, we sanction the innermost thoughts and drives of many of our fellowmen and fellowwomen to have sex *and* sex-love relations. If we take the opposing view, we hardly destroy these innermost thoughts and drives, but frequently tend to intensify them while denying them open and honest outlet. This, as Freud (1924-50, 1938) pointed out, is one of the main (though by no means the only) source of rampant neurosis.

4. I firmly believe that sex is a biological, as well as a social, drive, and that in its biological phases it is essentially non-affectional. If this is so, then we can expect

that, however we try to civilize the sex drives—and civilize them to *some* degree we certainly must—there will always be an underlying tendency for them to escape from our society-inculcated shackles and to be still partly felt in the raw.

When so felt, when our biosocial sex urges lead us to desire and enjoy sex without (as well as with) love, I do not see why we should make their experiencers feel needlessly guilty.

5. Many individuals—many millions in our society, I am afraid—have little or no capacity for affection or love. The majority of these individuals, perhaps, are emotionally disturbed, and should preferably be helped to increase their affectional propensities. But a large number are not particularly disturbed, and instead are neurologically or cerebrally deficient.

Mentally deficient persons, for example, as well as many dull normals (who, together, include several million citizens of our nation) are notoriously shallow in their feelings, and probably intrinsically so. Since these kinds of individuals—like the neurotic and the organically deficient—are for the most part, in our day and age, *not* going to be properly treated and *not* going to overcome their deficiencies, and since most of them definitely *do* have sex desires, I again see no point in making them guilty when they have nonloving sex relations.

Surely these unfortunate individuals are sufficiently handicapped by their disturbances or impairments without our adding to their woes by anathematizing them when they manage to achieve some nonamative sexual release.

6. Under some circumstances—though these, I admit, may be rare—some people find more satisfaction in nonloving coitus even though, under other circumstances, these *same* people may find more satisfaction in sex-love affairs. Thus, the man who *normally* enjoys being with his girlfriend because he loves as well as is sexually attracted to her, may occasionally find immense satisfaction in being with another girl with whom he has distinctly nonloving relations.

Granting that this may be (or is it?) unusual, I do not see why it should be condemnable.

7. If many people get along excellently and most cooperatively with business partners, employees, professors, laboratory associates, acquaintances, and even spouses for whom they have little or no love or affection, but with whom they have certain specific things in common, I do not see why there cannot be individuals who get along excellently and most cooperatively with sex mates with whom they may have little else in common.

I personally can easily see the tragic plight of a man who spends much time with a girl with whom he has nothing in common but sex: since I believe that life is too short to be well consumed in relatively one-track or intellectually low-level pursuits. I would also think it rather unrewarding for a girl to spend much time with a male with whom she had mutually satisfying sex, friendship, and cultural interests but no love involvement. This is because I would like to see people, in their 70-odd years of life, have maximum rather than minimum satisfactions with individuals of the other sex with whom they spend considerable time.

I can easily see, however, even the most intelligent and highly cultured individuals spending a *little* time with members of the other sex with whom they have common sex and cultural but no real love interests. And I feel that, for the time expended in this manner, their lives may be immeasurably enriched.

Moreover, when I encounter friends or psychotherapy clients who become enamored and spend considerable time and effort thinking about and being with a member of the other sex with whom they are largely sexually obsessed, and for whom they have little or no love, I mainly view these sexual infatuations as one of the penalties of their being human. For humans are the kind of animals who are easily disposed to this type of behavior (Grant, 1957).

I believe that one of the distinct inconveniences or tragedies of human sexuality is that it endows us, and perhaps particularly the males among us, with a propensity to become exceptionally involved and infatuated with members of the other sex whom, had we no sex urges, we would hardly notice. That is too bad; and it might well be a better world if it were otherwise. But it is *not* otherwise, and I think it is silly and pernicious for us to condemn ourselves because we are the way that we are in this respect.

We had better *accept* our biosocial tendencies, or our fallible humanity—instead of constantly blaming ourselves and futilely trying to change certain of its relatively harmless, though still somewhat tragic, aspects.

For reasons such as these, I feel that although it is usually—if not always—*desirable* for human beings to have sex relations with those they love rather than with those they do not love, it is by no means *necessary* that they do so. When we teach that it *is* necessary, we only needlessly condemn millions of our citizens to self-blame and atonement.

The position which I take—that there are several good reasons why affectional, as against non-affectional, sex relations are desirable but not necessary—can be assailed on several counts. I shall now consider some of the objections to this position to see if they cannot be effectively answered.

It may be said that an individual who has non-loving instead of loving sex relations is not necessarily wicked but that he is self-defeating because, while going for immediate gratification, he will miss out on even greater enjoyments. But this would only be true if such an individual (whom we shall assume, for the sake of discussion, *would* get greater enjoyment from affectional sex relations than from non-affectional ones) were *usually* or *always* having non-affectionate coitus. If he were *occasionally* or *sometimes* having love with sex, and the rest of the time having sex without love, he would be missing out on very little, if any, enjoyment.

72

Under these circumstances, in fact, he would normally get *more* pleasure from *sometimes* having sex without love. For the fact remains, and must not be unrealistically ignored, that in our present-day society sex without love is *much more frequently* available than sex with love.

Consequently, to ignore non-affectional coitus when affectional coitus is not available would, from the standpoint of enlightened self-interest, be sheer folly. In relation both to immediate *and* greater enjoyment, the individual would thereby be losing out.

The claim can be made of course that if an individual sacrifices sex without love *now* he will experience more pleasure by having sex with love in the future. This is an interesting claim; but I find no empirical evidence to sustain it. In fact, on theoretical grounds it seems most unlikely that it will be sustained. It is akin to the claim that if an individual starves himself for several days in a row he will greatly enjoy eating a meal at the end of a week or a month. I am sure he will—provided that he is then not too sick or debilitated to enjoy anything! But, even assuming that such an individual derives enormous satisfaction from his one meal a week or a month, is his *total* satisfaction greater than it would have been had he enjoyed three good meals a day for that same period of time? I doubt it.

So with sex. Anyone who starves himself sexually for a long period of time—as virtually everyone who rigidly sticks to the sex with love doctrine must—will (perhaps) *ultimately* achieve greater satisfaction when

73

he does find sex with love than he would have had, had he been sexually freer. But, even assuming that this is so, will his *total* satisfaction be greater?

It may be held that if both sex with and without love are permitted in any society, the non-affectional sex will drive out affectional sex, somewhat in accordance with Gresham's laws of currency. On the contrary, however, there is much reason to believe that just because an individual has sex relations, for quite a period, on a non-affectional basis, he will be more than eager to replace it, eventually, with sex with love.

From my clinical experience, I have often found that males who most want to settle down to having a single mistress or wife are those who have tried numerous lighter affairs and found them wanting. The view that sex without love eradicates the need for affectional sex relationships is somewhat akin to the ignorance is bliss theory. For it virtually says that if people never experienced sex with love they would never realize how good it was and therefore would never strive for it.

Or else the proponents of this theory seem to be saying that sex without love is so greatly satisfying, and sex with love so intrinsically difficult and disadvantageous to attain, that given the choice between the two, most people would pick the former. If this is so, then by all means let them pick the former—with which, in terms of their greater and total happiness, they would presumably be better off.

I doubt, however, that this hypothesis *is* factually sustainable. From clinical experience, again, I can say that individuals who are capable of sex with love usually seek and find it; while those who remain non-affectional in their sex affairs generally are not particularly capable of sex with love and need psychotherapeutic help before they can become thus capable.

Although, as a therapist, I frequently work with individuals who are only able to achieve non-affectional sex affairs and, through helping them eliminate their irrational fears and blockings, make it possible for them to achieve sex-love relationships, I still would doubt that *all* persons who take no great pleasure in sex with love are emotionally deficient. Some quite effective individuals—such as Immanuel Kant, for instance—seem to be so wholeheartedly dedicated to *things* or *ideas* that they rarely or never become amatively involved with people.

As long as such individuals have vital, creative interests and are intensely absorbed or involved with *something*, I would hesitate to diagnose them as being necessarily neurotic merely because they do not ordinarily become intensely absorbed with *people*. Some of these non-lovers of human beings are, of course, emotionally disturbed. But *all?* I wonder.

Disturbed or not, I see no reason why individuals who are dedicated to things or ideas should not have, in many or most instances, perfectly normal sex drives. And, if they do, I fail to see why they should not consummate their sex urges in non-affectional ways in order to have more time and energy for their non-amative pursuits.

75

It may be objected that man's sex drives are not merely biological, but *biosocial;* and that some restrictions, such as the banning on non-affectional sex relations, have to be put on them in order to make for the common good. This, to some extent, is certainly true. Man should, in fact must, inhibit his sex drives in certain respects if he is to live with his fellows in a cooperative, social manner.

The question is, however: Should man's self-imposed social-sexual restrictions be minimal or maximal?

Certainly, human beings should not rape members of the other sex; pretend that they love to win sex favors; take sexual advantage of minors; etc. But, assuming that two adult humans, who are being perfectly honest with each other, *want* to have non-loving sex relations for a day, a year, or forever—what is uncooperative, anti-social, or harmful about *that?*

From a cultural or conditioning point of view, there is little doubt that most men and women *can* be raised so that they come to desire sex only when it is accompanied by love and become guilty about their non-affectional sex affairs. Certainly they *can* be—but why *should* they?

My thesis, however, is quite the opposite: namely, that sex with instead of without love *may* for *some* people be *preferable* rather than *necessary;* and that forcing a sex-love philosophy and activity on *all* people will most probably lead to *less* human happiness and *more* emotional disturbance.

It may be alleged that if human beings have non-affectional coitus their sex activity will be alienated from and unacceptable to the rest of their personality, and that therefore they will develop severe internal conflicts. The answer to this is that such conflicts do not exist innately but are almost entirely *created* by unscientific sex teachings—such as the teaching that sex without love is pointless or wicked.

Without this kind of sex teaching, some individuals might have *mild* conflicts between sexually enjoying themselves in a non-affectional manner or waiting until a full-blown love affair between them and a suitable partner ensued. But if we did not deliberately *teach* people that sex without love is unjustified or worthless, I am sure that *most* of their conflicts concerning this kind of behavior would vanish.

It may be contended that if love without sex were not discouraged or proscribed, an increase in adultery would occur. Assuming that such an increase would be undesirable, I would again hypothesize the reverse proposition: namely that the greater the emphasis there is on the idea that sex must only be had with love, the greater tendency there will be for men and women to commit adultery.

This is because in many or most American marriages, for reasons which I need not go into at the moment, little love seems to remain after the first few years. But sex relations, for the most part, continue. If these sex relations without love were to stop, as the proponents of the sex-must-be-had-with-love theory presumably should advocate, then literally millions of husbands and wives who have been married for, say, ten or more years would be driven to adultery—where it is probable that many would find, at least for a while, sex with love.

The notion that sex must be accompanied by love is a rather romantic notion that does not square well with modern sociological concepts of marriage, since most of the experts in the field keep writing that marriage, in order to be lastingly happy should be somewhat de-romanticized. Both romantic love and sex satisfaction, I would say, are most easily maintained if the individual who seeks them changes his or her partners frequently. Consequently, if one *insists* that love and sex must go together, one thereby virtually dooms the continuation of millions of marriages that now, albeit none too ecstatically, are maintained.

It is sometimes held that since the value of coitus without affection is exceptionally small compared to the value of coitus with affection, the former should be discouraged in favor of the latter. This is an exceptionally weak argument because, in my estimation (as well, apparently, as that of literally millions of other humans), coitus without affection has a very strong, positive value in, of, by, and for itself; and the fact that coitus with affection may have a still stronger, more positive value for some or most individuals should not be used to denigrate the value of sex without love.

I personally feel that a fine steak or a chunk of roast pork is distinctly more nutritious and satisfying than a box of candy; but I would hardly try to turn people against eating sweets. If anyone thinks that candy is better than steak, that is his value, and though I disagree with it, I respect it as a value different from my own.

Similarly, if millions of people think that sex without love is as good as or better than sex with love, I again disagree with but respect their evaluation. Maybe they would be better off if they gave up loveless sex for sex with affection; but I, for one, am not going to try to force them to do so.

It may be objected that it is the responsibility of social thinkers and public officials to raise the standards of the populace, for the greater good and enjoyment of this populace; and that therefore sex with affection should be highly touted while affectionless sexuality should be scorned and banned. To this objection to sex without love I would offer several points of rebuttal:

1. Granting—for the sake of discussion—that people might be better off if they raised their standards of sexual participation, the question is: Should they be *forced* to do so?

Many Americans would doubtlessly be happier and better occupied if they listened to classical music and viewed Shakespearean plays on TV than if they listened to popular music and viewed quiz shows. But does this mean that we should jail the rock-and-roll addicts or make the quiz show viewers feel thoroughly ashamed of themselves?

A psychological colleague recently asked me what was my attitude toward forced conciliation when people come to court for marital difficulties. I replied that (a) I definitely thought, on the basis of my experience, that individuals who are forced into psychotherapy or counseling can often, even though it is at first against their will, learn to benefit from this counseling and thus save their marriages; but that (b) I would not, under any circumstances, want to have them *forced*, either by direct coercion or making them terribly guilty, into resorting to conciliation. I am more— perhaps idealistically—attached to the notion of the value of human individuality and freedom than I am to the notion of forcing people to be "better" than they presumably are.

I am also reminded, in this connection, of a recent talk by an authority on criminology, who pointed out that in dictatorships they invariably have much less gangsterism and criminality, in the usual sense of these terms, than we have in our kind of democracy. The question he raised was: Is the social cost of such "benefits" too high? I think it is.

Even, then, were I firmly convinced that humans would be better off if they refrained from loveless sex affairs and only confined themselves to loving ones, I would balk at coercing them into following my belief. The "cure" in this instance would, I am afraid, be worse than the "disease."

2. Assuming that it might be better if men and women refrained from coitus without affection, the fact is that such a general change in human behavior is not going to take place for decades or centuries to come. In

80

the meantime, whether we like it or not, we are going to continue to live in a world where countless individuals *do* have and enjoy loveless sex affairs. If this is so, why should we create needless guilt and despair among the residents of our *existing* society by scorning or penalizing them for having sex without love?

3. Although I personally prefer classical to popular music and Hamlet to quiz shows, I would hate to see a world in which there was *no* popular music or quiz programs. Even highly intelligent, educated, and cultured individuals, I am sure, will *sometimes* want to listen to or view "cheap" entertainment. Similarly, even people who *largely* enjoy sex with affection will, I feel, *sometimes* thoroughly, even ecstatically, enjoy sex without affection. And why should they not?

It is often contended that, because America is a basically puritanical country, it will never accept sex without affection; and that therefore, rather than condemn young people to abstinence before marriage, we should encourage them to accept sex with affection—which, presumably, the nation as a whole will tolerate. This, it seems to me, is a rather defeatist position. The fact is that where many highly respectable Americans now are able to accept sex with but not without love, a half century ago the same kind of Americans were only able to accept sex with marriage and viewed all non-marital relations, however lovingly based, as despicable and worthless (Reiss, 1960).

If, in the course of the last half century, such a drastic change has taken place in our sex mores that affectional

81

non-marital relations are now being accepted where they previously were thoroughly condemned, there is no reason to believe that in the course of the next half century non-affectional non-marital relations may not become equally acceptable.

The argument that because something is not now socially approved, and that therefore people who engage in this disapproved act will get into difficulties and would be more sensible to refrain, is tautological. Of course people who perform socially unsanctioned actions will find themselves criticized and, sometimes, penalized. The question we are discussing, however, is not whether those who have sex without love in present-day America will be socially disapproved; but *should* they be?

As noted above, the fact seems to be that from an *individual* viewpoint, loveless sex affairs would seem to be deemed exceptionally desirable by myriads of contemporary males and females—otherwise, it is difficult to see why they go to such great lengths to have them. From a *social* viewpoint, however, the fact is also clear that our customs and mores seriously condemn such unaffectional affairs. The question therefore arises: Are the social, and much flouted rules, legitimate, sane ones?

The liberal proponents of the sex-should-be-had-only-with-love theory hold that the social interdictions against loveless sex are legitimate because (a) sex is far better with than without love and (b) people should be encouraged or forced to see this.

THE JUSTIFICATION OF SEX WITHOUT LOVE

In regard to point (a), they may have a reasonable argument—if only they would modify it to read: Sex is far better with than without love for *some* or *most* individuals under *some* or *most* circumstances. In regard to point (b), they have a far less cogent argument. For even assuming that affectional affairs are usually or often preferable to non-affectional ones for the majority of men and women, it is still questionable whether those who benightedly fail to see this should be "encouraged" or coerced into seeing the light by emotional blackmail, guilt-producing exhortations, and threats of severe social or legal penalties.

If the goodness of sex with love (or any other mode of human behavior) cannot be effectively propagated without this kind of verbal and statutory bludgeoning, it is to be seriously wondered just how "good" it really is in the first place and how "beneficent" are the tactics of its do-gooder adherents in the second place.

Rather than go along with the well-meaning but dubiously well-handled views of the upholders of the sex-must-be-wedded-to-love theory, I would much prefer to take my stand with Voltaire. Although I may not personally favor sex without love to affectional sex affairs, I shall fight for the rights of those who do.

6.

Why Americans Are So Fearful of Sex

In the whole wide world there is probably no large group of people who are so fearful of sex as are we Americans.

The southern Europeans, such as the French and the Italians, are notoriously freer about many of their sex ways than we are (Van Emde Boas, 1961). The northern Europeans, especially the Scandinavians, are often so enlightened about sex that they tolerate illegitimacy on the one hand and homosexuality on the other (Bohm and Johnstadt, 1961). The North Africans tend to live in what we would consider a hotbed of sexual vice (Edwardes and Masters, 1962).

Most Central African and Southern African natives have many customs, including polygamy, which we would look upon with horror (de Rachewiltz, 1961). Oriental and Middle East sex beliefs and practices are so much freer than ours in many ways that our modern sex manuals are beginning just recently to catch up with some of the knowledge which for centuries has been recorded in Persian, Hindu, and Chinese texts (Gichner, 1957, 1958; Malla, 1964; Nefzawi, 1964).

Even the English, from whom our Anglo-Saxon codes of sex conduct primarily stem, are in many ways less fearful of sex than are we. English newspapers and magazines publish details of sex crimes and happenings which would never be allowed in their American equivalents. English sex manuals are not only more outspoken than American sex books but have a proportionately wider sale. The premarital and extramarital behavior of the English girls, as many of our GIs discovered during the last world war, is in many respects significantly less inhibited than that of our own girls (Epton, 1962).

We Americans have a deceptively free exterior attitude about sex; but underneath we are chicken. We pet, as the Kinsey reports show, almost universally. We engage, to a considerable degree, in masturbatory, fornicative, adulterous, homosexual, and other types of sex outlets. But we usually do so queasily, stealthily, guiltily. We cannot help our actions, as it were, but we

85

can help our thoughts—and we do help them drive us to anxiety, despair, neurosis. We have our sexual cake, but we don't really eat it—or we gulp it down in such a manner as to bring on acute indigestion.

The result is considerable frigidity on the part of our females, varying degrees of impotence on the part of our males, and enormous amounts of dissatisfaction, unappeased hunger, and continual sex fear on the part of both (Arlington, 1958; Reich, 1962).

Why?

Why should I and other psychotherapists have to spend so much of our time seeing a continuous succession of disturbed people, most of whom have some serious degree of sexual anxiety?

There are several important answers to these whys:

1. *Americans are specifically taught to be fearful of sex.* During their childhood and adolescence, all the possible dangers, and virtually none of the pleasures, of human sexuality are drummed into their heads and hearts. Grim specters of loss of reputation, illegitimate pregnancy, illegal abortion, syphilis, gonorrhea, perversion, physical and emotional breakdown, etc. are ceaselessly thrown at them while they are growing up.

The idea that sex is good, sex is fun, sex is one of the greatest and most repeatable of human joys is rarely unequivocally brought to their attention. In jokes, yes; in sly asides, of course; in under-the-counter pamphlets and books, certainly. In these indirect and backhanded ways the idea that sex is good, hot, and spicy is slammed across to the average American male and female. But directly and forthrightly? Heavens, no! From these respectable sources come cavilings, quibblings, cautionings.

The result, as I noted in my book *The Folklore of Sex,* is that the American boy and girl, and later the American man and woman, believe that sex is good—*and* bad; tasty—*and* nasty. They are, in a word, conflicted. And conflict means indecision and doubt—which means fear.

2. *Americans are raised to be overly-competitive about sex.* Our boys and girls are made to feel that, above all else, they must succeed, achieve, win out in the social-sexual game. They must not merely enjoy themselves on their dates and eventually achieve good marriages—nay, they must date the *best* boy or girl in the neighborhood; be the *finest* lover for miles around; have the *greatest* home and family (Riesman, 1961).

Americans must do all these things, moreover, without any experience to speak of, sans any notable period of learning. If they study arithmetic, French, or engineering, they are of course expected to take a while to get onto the subject, to learn it. But if they study what is perhaps the most complicated subject in the world—namely, that of getting along well with a member of the other sex—they are somehow supposed to be able to discover all the answers with no learning experience whatever and to make the best possible impression literally from scratch. This, of course, they usually cannot do. They naturally make a certain amount of blunders, errors, mistakes. But each error is considered to be an unforgivable crime. Each time when he misses her mouth and kisses her nose, or she goes a little too far or not far enough in petting, or either of them fails to say the right romantic word when the moon is full: each mistake is considered catastrophic, disastrous (Ellis, 1962a).

This means that the boy and girl soon become afraid to try certain actions or chance certain words. Then, not acquiring any experience or familiarity with taking these actions or saying these words, they become afraid of taking or saying them in the future. Thus arises a vicious circle, where dire fear of making a social-sexual mistake leads to lack of learning, which in turn leads to further fear of ineptness, which in turn leads to further inhibition of learning, and so on to a hopeless eternity.

This also means that when the boys and girls who keep fruitlessly merry-go-rounding in this manner finally do stumble into marriage, they still have learned relatively little about social-sexual relations, and carry their fears and restraints into their marital relationship.

3. *Americans are brought up to fear tenderness and love.* American males, in particular, are raised to be "regular guys" and to avoid "sissified" displays of emotionality. They do not kiss, like the French; throw their arms around like the Italians; act very warm to their children, like many peoples of the world. Even Ameri-

can women are often raised so that they are ashamed to cry openly, to laugh uproariously, to let their hair down in public.

This means that, in spite of our Hollywood films and romantic novels, we do not allow ourselves to be overly warm, affectionate, loving. We often, in fact, try to use sex as a substitute for love: to throw ourselves into a wild necking session because it is easier to say with our hands what we would be embarrassed to say with our lips.

But love inhibition breeds sex inhibition. As we inhibit and deaden our tender reactions, we also block some of our deepest sex sensations. Love, moreover, is an exceptionally good antidote for all kinds of fear; and to the extent that we have little love, we tend to have more fear—including sex fear.

4. *Americans are generally fearful and often neurotic.* We Americans tend to have unreasonable goals and ideals, especially in regard to worldly success and keeping up with the Joneses. We frequently are never weaned from our childhood ideas of grandiosity and refuse to face the harsh realities of life and accept the world as it is. We have seriously conflicting values and philosophies of life—such as the notion that we should be good and kind, on the one hand, and ruthlessly make a million dollars on the other.

Because of our general insecurities, immaturities, and conflicts, we tend to be beset with multitudinous feelings of doubt and inadequacy; and these often lap

89

over into our sexual attitudes. Where general neurosis is epidemic, sexual disturbance cannot be too far away.

Assuming that Americans, because of reasons like the foregoing, are probably the most sexually fearful of any large group of people in the world, the question arises: Can anything effective be done to make us less panicky in this respect? Certainly: but only if the problem is tackled in all its important ramifications, and not treated as if it were a simple sex problem alone.

On an individual basis, there are several things which a sexually fearful individual may do if he wants to overcome his disturbances:

First: he can frankly admit to himself that he is sexually fearful, and not try to hide his fear beneath a mask of false sophistication. He can honestly acknowledge that he has sex problems, instead of cavalierly attempting to dismiss them.

Second: he can obtain all possible objective information about sex, particularly in relation to his own fears. He can learn, from modern sex manuals and from talks with a physician or psychologist, some of the essential truths about masturbation, sexual inadequacy, sex deviation, and other aspects of human sexuality which he may illogically and ignorantly fear.

Third: he can sometimes do some of the sex acts of which he is irrationally afraid. He can experiment with coital or extracoital techniques which he theoretically knows are normal and healthy, but which he superstitiously or bigotedly believes are "bad" or "wicked."

Fourth: he can begin consistently to indoctrinate

himself *against* some of his senseless sex fears, instead
of continually reinfecting himself with them. He can
keep telling himself, over and over again, that acts like
autoerotism are *not* wrong, *not* childish, *not* harmful.
He can tell himself, instead, that sex behavior which
does not needlessly and definitely harm others, and
that is not fetishistically or compulsively performed by
himself, is good, harmless, and beneficial, and should
be practiced as much as he normally wants.

Fifth: if an individual tries all the foregoing techniques of helping himself over his own sex fears, and he
still finds that he is seriously possessed by them, he
should not hesitate to go for psychological help. The
chances are, in such a case, that he has a general or a
psychological neurosis, and that he may be significantly
improved or cured by going for intensive psychotherapy.

On a social basis, a concerted attack on the all-per-
vasive sex fears that now inhabit and inhibit our populace is certainly most necessary at the present time and
is possible in the following terms:

1. Our society should put an end to virtually all sex
censorship. Such censorship certainly does not prevent
the public from seeing the material that is officially
banned—indeed, it invariably encourages the distribution of this material. What it does do is, by its
very existence, make both fearful *and* enticing considerable sex behavior that, if it were freely permitted and
discussed, would be considered routine and less desirable.

2. We should objectify and minimize our antisexual laws. At most, as noted by Dr. Ralph Brancale and me in our book, *The Psychology of Sex Offenders,* we should only punish by law those sex acts which involve the use of force or duress; or an adult's taking sexual advantage of a minor; or public sex acts which are distasteful to the majority of those in whose presence they are committed. All acts other than these, which are engaged in privately between two competent adults, should not be subject to legal penalties.

3. We should, as outlined in Chapter 10 of this volume, give wholehearted attention to realistic sex education of our children, and should at all school and home levels, raise these children to understand the salient objective facts of human sexuality.

4. We should establish a number of sex institutes and clinics where irrationally fearful individuals may go for intensive treatment and where the best psychological investigation of and care for their problems would be possible.

5. We should particularly encourage and make suitable financial appropriations for considerable sexual research into some of the most important areas where illogical and unnecessary fear is now rampant.

If a concerted attack were made, along the foregoing individual and social lines, on the problem of sexual fear in our culture, it would be almost certain that such fear, if it did not entirely disappear, would at least be enormously reduced. Is the game, despite its difficulties, worth the candle? Or shall the defeatists among us, as they so often do, again win by default?

7.

Adventures with Sex Censorship

When I began my series for *The Independent* with a column tilted "New Light on Masturbation," Lyle Stuart wrote an editorial about the difficulties I had previously had trying to publish that material. Let me now recount some of my other first-hand adventures with sex censorship.

My serious encounters with restrictions on the publication of sex material began when I contracted to write my first book, *The Folklore of Sex*. Mr. Charles Boni asked me to do this book for him; and, since he did

not directly publish books himself, said that he would
arrange to do so through one of the large publishers, as
he had several times done before.

He accordingly submitted the outline of the book to
Simon and Schuster, with whom he had excellent relations. He was told that they had got into some difficulties on a sex book they had published some twenty
years previously, and that therefore it was their policy
to touch no works in this field. Shortly thereafter,
however, Simon and Schuster contracted to publish
Abraham Franzblau's *The Road to Sexual Maturity*—
surely one of the most reactionary books on sex brought
out in recent years.

Nothing daunted, Mr. Boni took the outline of *The
Folklore of Sex* to the world's largest publishers, Doubleday, who were quite enthusiastic about it and immediately contracted to publish the book. They were equally
delighted with the manuscript and were so eager to
send it to press that they arranged to do some of the re-
typing in their own offices.

Everything was set for publication in the fall of 1950
and galley and page proofs were speedily printed and
corrected. The imprint on the title page was that of
Doubleday & Company; and on the back of the title
page was the usual statement found in all Doubleday
books: "Printed in the United States at the Country
Life Press, Garden City, N.Y."

Then something happened.

"Certain people" at Doubleday began to get quite
distressed about the nature of the book when they

were shown the page proofs. Their distress appeared to stem from the facts that the book took a (rather mildly) liberal attitude toward sex; that it quoted from the most popular American newspapers and magazines, whose editors might object to having their sexual proclivities exposed; and that it also ruthlessly revealed the frankly sexual underpinnings of numerous best-selling novels and non-fictional works, many of which were either published by Doubleday or distributed by one of the several book clubs owned by Doubleday.

After several frantic conferences were held, publication of *The Folklore of Sex* was delayed; Doubleday's name was taken off the title page and Charles Boni's name substituted instead; publication was still further delayed; and the book finally appeared almost a half year after its originally planned publication date.

It was still printed at the Country Life Press and was distributed by Doubleday. But although editorial enthusiasm for it was sustained, and Mr. Boni did everything possible to aid its sale, promotional initiative at Doubleday noticeably dimmed.

Few reviews or publicity stories appeared in leading newspapers and magazines; The *New York Times* and The *Chicago Tribune* were not seriously opposed when they refused to publish any ads whatever on the book; and the volume was remaindered with unusual alacrity. Only when, a decade later, Grove Press published a revised edition of the book in paperback form, did it began to attain real popularity.

So much for *The Folklore of Sex*.

My second book, *The American Sexual Tragedy,* was something of a sequel to the first book but Doubleday, who had an option to publish it, didn't even want to look at the manuscript. It was then accepted by Twayne Publishers, who had no vested interests in well-known authors or book clubs, and who were unusually liberal in their editing of the manuscript.

Where Doubleday had insisted that I take out several references to best-selling writers or famous personalities —such as my highlighting of several sadistic passages in Frank Slaughter's novel, *Divine Mistress*—Twayne wielded no blue pencil in this respect. They did object, however, to my dedicating the volume "to John Ciardi, one hell of a fine editor," insisting that this was not a dignified remark for a Ph.D. in psychology to make. I disagreed; but they won. Again, Lyle Stuart and Grove Press had to come to the rescue later by including the original dedication in the revised edition of the book.

My third book, *Sex Life of the American Woman and the Kinsey Report,* ran into serious censorship trouble again. Greenberg contracted to publish the work and then arranged with Popular Library to bring out a paper-backed edition simultaneously with their hardcover edition.

When Popular Library saw the manuscript of this anthology, they first rejected two of the chapters, one which I had written on masturbation and another on prostitution with which I had collaborated with Dr. Harry Benjamin. Then, after further hemming and hawing, they reneged on their contract to publish the whole work, even though they had to sacrifice a substantial down payment by so doing.

Although Popular Library's objections, like those of Doubleday, were never made too explicit, it appeared that they ardently disliked the fact that *Sex Life of the American Woman* was largely pro-Kinsey and they were afraid that, as a paperback publisher, they might run into official censorship on the book.

Doubleday, out of similar fears, had deliberately overpriced *The Folklore of Sex*, the argument being that official and semi-official agencies are less likely to ban a book that is high-priced than one that is low-priced. Actually, for all the publishers' caution in this connection, none of my publications has as yet aroused any official action, except when a paperback edition of *Sex Without Guilt* was banned, along with 99 other books (including novels by Faulkner, Steinbeck, and O'Hara) in one county of Southern California.

Sex Life of the American Woman and the Kinsey Report was finally published in hard-backed form by Greenberg, a firm that itself took a highly liberal attitude toward the publication of sex material. As a result of legal advice, however, Greenberg omitted from the book the same two chapters that Popular Library had first banned.

My opinion, and that of my collaborators on the book, was that these chapters were not objectionable or censorable. We lost.

With my fourth book, *Sex, Society and the Individual*, I ran into no censorship problems as far as publication and editing were concerned: for the simple reason that the book was published by Dr. A. P. Pillay, the co-editor of the work.

The New York Times, however, for several years refused to publish advertisements on this or any of my sex books—even if the ad contained nothing more than the title of the book and the name of the author. At first, large advertisers like Marboro Books, who include scores of titles in each ad, were able to squeeze mentions of some of my volumes into their *Times* displays. But later even this privilege was denied all sex books in my authorship.

When queried in this respect, the *Times* never came up with a satisfactory explanation—especially in view of the fact that it frequently publishes advertisements for more conservatively attuned sex volumes. During the last several years, the *Times* has run ads on several of my sex books, but has often insisted on cutting out large chunks of the ads submitted for *The Art and Science of Love, Sex and the Single Man,* and other books of my authorship.

With my fifth book on sexual topics, *The Psychology of Sex Offenders* (Ellis and Brancale, 1956), which was published by Charles C Thomas, I encountered no censorship difficulties. Thomas is a medical publisher, and its editors did not object to a single word or sentence in the volume. And since the book was never published in a paperback edition or offered for display in The *New York Times* or any other popular paper or magazine, it managed to run into no censorship troubles.

ADVENTURES WITH SEX CENSORSHIP

Most of my subsequent works on sex, love, and marriage have been published by Lyle Stuart, Inc.—largely because, after this firm brought out the first edition of *Sex Without Guilt*, I discovered that the same freedom of speech which permeates the columns of *The Independent* similarly prevails in Lyle's book publications. Although he has personally disagreed with some of my ultraliberal views (after all, he has been raising a teenage daughter of his own during the past several years!), he has never red-penciled any of my frank expressions or expletives; and, so far, both of us have nicely managed to stay out of jail.

In any event, even though my most controversial books—including *Creative Marriage, Reason and Emotion in Psychotherapy, If This Be Sexual Heresy* . . . , *Sex and the Single Man, The Intelligent Woman's Guide to Manhunting, Homosexuality: Its Causes and Cure*—and my hard-hitting sex manual, *The Art and Science of Love* have all been published by Lyle Stuart, Inc., and even though reviewers have frequently uttered anguished screams about my ideas and language in these books, my censorship problems with them have been absolutely nil. All of which tends to show, I am convinced, that it is not the American public and our gendarmerie which are our worst censoring agencies; it is usually the publishers themselves.

Just to make this point even more convincing, I have recently had the same old censorship mish-mash again when I arranged to have some sex books brought out by other publishers than Lyle Stuart. Bernard Geis commissioned me to do *The Intelligent Woman's Guide to Manhunting,* liked the manuscript very much, but found my language "too rough." When I reluctantly agreed to tone some of it down, so that the book would not be inordinately delayed in going to press, he finally decided that his main business associates (which include *Look* and *Esquire* magazines and Art Linkletter) would never tolerate the liberal sex views I included in the book, especially those outlined in a section on "The fine art of the pickup." Although he predicted (with what subsequently turned out to be a goodly degree of accuracy) that the book would sell very well, he forfeited the advance royalty, returned the manuscript to me, and agreed to let me have—guess who!—publish it.

A little later on, I took another chance and let Julian Messner, Inc. talk me (and my associate, Edward Sagarin) into doing a book called *Nymphomania: A Study of the Oversexed Woman.* Much to our chagrin, some of the material in the manuscript was bowdlerized as it was being rushed into print; and the sexiest chapter in the book, which was called "How to Satisfy a Nymphomaniac Sexually" and which had been specifically asked for by the original editor, was entirely deleted because it was "too provocative." At the present writing, arrangements are being made to include this chapter in another of my books—whose publisher, this time, thinks it perfectly fine and proper.

With still another of my books—the massive, two-volumed *Encyclopedia of Sexual Behavior* which I edited in collaboration with Albert Abarbanel and

100

which was published by Hawthorn Books, Inc., the contents of the articles themselves were not censored by the publisher (except, I believe, in some of the foreign countries where the *Encyclopedia* has been translated and republished); but great effort was brought to bear on me and my collaborator to include in the volumes several ultraconservative articles, since a number of our contributors were (without my instructing them to be) so liberal in their presentations.

Having, by now, published fifteen books on sex in an equal number of years, and having had considerable experience with many varieties of publishers, editors, reviewers, and advertising managers during this period, I am inclined to take a somewhat less than enthusiastic view of the many friends and fellow writers who greet me with some variation of "My God, aren't you lucky to be writing in the sex field. Such a popular area! And so much money to be made in it!"

Actually, this is largely bosh. Perhaps the cheap and sensational writers on sex, on the one hand, or the mealy-mouthed romanticists on the other hand, sell their talents for a pretty penny. Perhaps. But the hard-headed, objective, straight-shooting purveyor of sex information is hardly in this boat. In fact, he's lucky to set sail at all.

It is my experience that today's author who writes an honest sex book will, in the first place, have difficulty in finding any publisher for his work. Then if he does find a publisher, he will usually have to fight his way through censorship difficulties with the publisher and

SEX WITHOUT GUILT

his editors and lawyers. Then he will find that the public notices and reviews he receives rarely are commensurate in quantity or quality to those of non-sexual volumes which he may have published.

To make matters still worse, he will often find that his book has been deliberately overpriced just because it deals with sex. He may be shocked to note that some of the finest bookstores refuse to display it prominently, especially in their windows. Many libraries, he will discover, refuse to purchase the book; or else, when they do purchase it, put it behind locked shelves and discourage reader interest in it. Finally, his books may run into official or semi-official disapproval, and may be banned from advertising columns, from the mails, from public sale in certain communities, or, in extreme cases, from any further printings.

The one good break which the writer of sex books is likely to have is to find that if and when his arduously produced and fought-for volume is finally remaindered —as it easily may be in dishearteningly record time—it is *then* likely to be prominently displayed in bookstores and advertisements—because, of course, it deals with S-E-X.

In view of these facts, most of which are intrinsically present in our nation, I am inclined to paraphrase the famous advice which *Punch* almost a century ago gave to men about to be married. Say I in this latter day version: "Advice to authors who are about to write a sex book: Don't."

Having discussed some of my encounters with cen-

102

sorship in the course of writing and publishing books on sexual topics, I shall now continue this gory saga with a few of my adventures with other aspects of sex restriction. First, as to professional journals. You might not think that scientific journals, which presumably are devoted only to the publication of fact and truth, would be particularly squeamish about sex articles. But you might be surprised.

The International Journal of Sexology was, until his early tragic death, valiantly and spiritedly edited by Dr. A. P. Pillay of Bombay, India. It had numerous brushes with sex censorship and was at times banned in several countries. Many years ago, when it was published under the name of *Marriage Hygiene,* its entry into the United States was barred, and a famous court case was fought, and won, in its behalf.

Nonetheless, although I was the American editor of the *Journal,* and Dr. Pillay was continually asking me to write papers for it, he refused to publish my article, "New Light on Masturbation," which was later printed in *The Independent.* He apologetically wrote me that such an outspoken article just could not be published in India, because it would offend the members of certain sectarian groups.

Another paper of mine—on masturbation among prisoners—was requested by the editor of *The Journal of Social Therapy,* the official publication of the Medical Correctional Association. Contrary to the usual procedure for scientific publication, I received no proofs on this article before it went to press. When I saw it in print, I was shocked to find that what I considered to be the most important and forceful paragraph in the paper, which forthrightly said that prison officials should, far from discouraging their charges from masturbating, be thankful that they have some normal outlet, was completely omitted.

After the journal containing this article had already been printed, the editor asked me whether I would like to have some corrections or additions made in it. I said that I certainly would; and that when the paper was reprinted, as it was supposed to be, in a monograph to be issued by the Federal Government as a handbook for prison officials, I would definitely like to see the *full* version published. Since then I have heard nothing from the editor—and nothing about the proposed monograph.

My experience with the editors of *Social Problems,* the official journal of the Society for the Study of Social Problems, was surprisingly similar—only worse. After the publication of the second Kinsey report, I was asked to contribute a paper on the report for a special issue of the journal, which was later to be republished in book form.

I wrote an article on "Female Sexual Response and Marital Relations" in which I showed that, whatever one may think of the Kinsey methodology, the last five chapters of *Sexual Behavior in the Human Female* are most important for an understanding of human sex relations. As usual, I minced few words about how, if they took the Kinsey material seriously, husbands and wives could employ extra-vaginal as well as vaginal techniques to achieve greater sex satisfaction.

Much to my horror, this article was considerably cut when it appeared in *Social Problems*—purely because, the editors insisted, of necessary space limitations. I soon discovered, however, that whereas my paper was cut to the bone, to become easily the shortest one published, several other papers, especially those which were thoroughly anti-Kinsey, were given plenty of space.

As in the case of the article in *The Journal of Social Therapy*, the editors of *Social Problems* asked me, *after* publication, whether I would like any changes or additions in the paper when it went into book covers. I immediately replied that I damned well would. Several months later, when the book had already gone to press, they phoned to tell me that, somehow, they had forgotten about my request to use the original version of my paper, and that it was now too late to do anything about it, so they would print the highly bowdlerized version.

But even this did not end the matter. A few weeks later, they called to say that the book had turned out to be too long and that therefore several papers, including mine, had to be dropped entirely. They were very sorry, but that's the way things were, and nothing could be done about it.

When the book actually appeared, under the title of *Sexual Behavior in American Society*, it proved to be a rather massive tome of 446 pages, which not only contained the original papers that had been published in the journal, but many other articles, virtually all of them anti-Kinsey, reprinted from various other sources. Conspicuously lacking, however, was only one paper from the original symposium—mine. Similarly, a paper I was asked to do for a text on criminality was found to contain too much sexy language in the therapeutic conversations I reported with actual offenders and was rejected.

So much for some of my encounters with professional publications. With popular magazines, my experience has been. as one might expect in this pressure-minded society, even more replete with sex censorship.

Time and again I have been called upon to prepare or outline articles by editors of mass circulation magazines, as *Look, Redbook,* and the *Ladies Home Journal.* But although I think I may safely say that I am generally considered to be one of America's outstanding authorities on sexual subjects, for many years not a single of my down-to-earth essays in the field appeared in a large national magazine. My efforts were somehow always found to be "too realistic," "too bold for our readers" or "overly controversial." A footnote was originally inserted at this point to the effect that *Esquire* had just broken the sex barrier by accepting one of my articles, *The Case for Polygamy,* for early publication. However, after paying me generously for the article, *Esquire* first delayed its publication and finally at the behest of one of the chief editors who found it "too strong," returned it to me. At the time the first edition of this book was published the escutcheon of any American mass circulation journal still remained completely unsullied by the inclusion of a sex article by the impure Dr. Albert Ellis.

When I finally did break into print in a small popular magazine a few years ago, largely because the editor was a good friend of mine to whom I had given several ideas on what kind of periodical he might publish, he enthusiastically accepted my first article and vaguely said that he might change it around a bit. I thought, naturally, that he would consult me about these changes.

To my surprise, he blithely changed some of the salient points of my article without consulting me; and each change was a distinct toning-down of any liberal sex views I may have included. Thus, I asked, in the course of a discussion of sex freedom in marriage, "Can the average American couple practice sex freedom in marriage and still have a good marital relationship?" And I replied: "The answer is, alas, no." My editor friend changed this to: "The answer is, of course, a resounding no."

Since the publication of the first edition of this book, I have had more success than usual with publishing material in national magazines. *Pageant* has been the most liberal periodical in this respect, and has actually asked me to write and has printed four sex articles by me. Mass circulation magazines such as *Cosmopolitan*, *This Week*, and *True Story*, have also included pieces of my authorship. More often than not, however, such publications have been more interested in my non-sexual than my sexual writings; and when they have run the latter they have commonly deleted or changed significant passages where I was exceptionally frank about copulatory or noncoital processes.

Even the highly sexy men's magazines have at times proved to be quite prissy in this regard. Thus, after I had written, on request, an article on nymphomania for *Gent* (which is normally one of the sexiest of the men's publications), the editor apologetically told me that he had to be very careful of post office regulations, and that I therefore had to delete all explicit references to sex relations that I had included in this article. And an article I wrote for another men's periodical, *Saga*, on "How to Have an Affair and End It with Style," was seriously cut and bowdlerized, without my consent, before it was printed.

Space does not permit the recounting of all my other brushes with restrictions on my written words on sex, so let me give some examples from the field of the spoken word.

I have often given talks on sexual topics, particularly to public forums, church, and community groups. Normally, I find that some members of my audience are somewhat startled, at the beginning of my talk, when I openly and unashamedly start using scientific sex terminology (such as "vagina," "penis," and "erection") and when I do not cavil about how they can achieve greater sex satisfaction by ridding themselves of many of their tabus, superstitions, and sex prejudices.

ADVENTURES WITH SEX CENSORSHIP

After a few minutes of my talking this way, however, I invariably find that the members of the audience acquire, by a kind of process of osmosis, some of my own lack of embarrassment and concern about unadulterated sexuality and become relaxed enough to enjoy, and even actively participate in, the discussion. After the formal presentation is over, many of them usually come up to speak to me informally, and sometimes keep me till far into the night or early morning.

If audience reaction is all to the good at these times, much less can be said for administrative response. For as soon as the sponsors of my sex talks get wind of how things are going, they frequently become most disturbed and block all efforts, which members of the audience often instigate, to have me return for further talks.

One of the most flagrant instances of administrative interference I have ever encountered occurred when I was talking to the members of a community group in the Bronx. The regular leader of the group had to leave before my speech was finished, but he left a specially chosen chairman in his place and, in addition, his wife to monitor the proceedings from a first-row vantage point.

I was talking, in this instance, about the contributions of modern sexual research to the husband-wife relationships. When the last word was hardly out of my mouth, the director's wife got up and made a twenty-minute peroration against almost everything I had said; and then, immediately after she finished, the chairman of the group, as if by a pre-arranged signal, himself gave a ten-minute speech which was largely directed against the points I had made, and then adjourned the meeting.

Several members of the audience, incensed at the fact that I was not even given a chance to rebut my two speaking associates, rose to object to the peremptory manner in which the meeting was being closed. The chairman, broadly insinuating that the objectors were ruffians, blackguards, and communists, still closed the meeting. Sexual virtue, no doubt, once more triumphed.

After I wrote the first edition of *Sex Without Guilt*, I began to make more frequent radio and TV performances; and I quickly began to run into censorship trouble in this sensitive medium. When I spoke up in favor of premarital sex relations almost a decade ago on Channel 5 in New York, such a hue and cry was raised that many years after that my appointment as a consultant in clinical psychology to the Veterans Administration was temporarily blocked because I had advocated "free love" on this particular program.

I appeared many times on the old Long John Nebel show on WOR, New York; and the programs on which I appeared were very popular and were normally tape recorded and rebroadcasted at a later date. The program I did on *Sex Without Guilt*, however, in which masturbation and fornication were specifically mentioned as desirable sex acts, was forbidden to be rebroadcast by the station management.

On radio station WINS I debated the virtues of premarital sex relations with the editor of a magazine (who stoutly opposed such relations, although she was unmarried herself at this time and showed up at the studio with a man who was obviously her lover). When I vigorously stated that a girl, to be mentally healthy, had damned well better stop caring too much what her associates thought of her reputation, there were hundreds of protests to the station; the Federal Communications Commission took the program off the air until the station explained that it had not specifically invited me to say what I said, and that I had made similar statements over many other radio and TV shows previously; and the management of the station humbly apologized to its audience, the next day, for my appearance.

On the David Susskind "Open End" TV show, I appeared with Max Lerner, Hugh Hefner, Ralph Ginzburg, Maxine Davis, and Reverend Arthur Kinsolving, in a two-hour program entitled "The Sex Revolution." When David Susskind asked me, on this program, what I would do if I had a teenage daughter, and when I candidly said that I would encourage her to pet to orgasm rather than to have intercourse (because of the danger of pregnancy involved in coitus), but that if she insisted on having full copulatory relations I would fit her up with a diaphragm or birth control pills and tell her to have fun, the program was banned from the Metropolitan Broadcasting syndicated TV network, and the two-hour TV tape was never played anywhere. Ironically enough, Max Lerner, on the same show, had previ-

111

ously remarked that the mere fact that we were doing this program that night showed how liberal in its sex attitudes TV was becoming!

When I did a daytime radio performance on WCBS New York on a show where I directly answered listeners who phoned in to talk to me while I was on the air, and when I clearly said that premarital sex relations were fine and that the Bible was hardly a good guide to sane sex conduct, more than a thousand listeners jammed the telephone lines to complain to the station about my sexual liberality; and the Federal Communications Commission again considered suspending this program from the air. When I said similar things on the telephone-answering shows on radio stations in Philadelphia, Boston, Los Angeles, and other cities, complaints again were voluble and vociferous; and in consequence I am now persona non grata with several of these stations.

In recent years, a pernicious form of precensorship has been applied to me by several radio and TV outlets. Thus, producers of the Barry Gray show, "To Tell the Truth," "Open Discussion," or some other program will call me and arrange to have me be on the air a week or two later. Then, just before the program is about to be recorded or to go on live, they will call me again and give some lame excuse why they cannot use me on the show, or else will honestly admit that they have been told that I am "too controversial" a figure, and that therefore someone connected with the program objects to my being on it.

ADVENTURES WITH SEX CENSORSHIP

As a result of these various types of sex censorship, my participations in radio and TV programs in New York City and throughout the country have been seriously curtailed in recent years, and I sometimes wonder if eventually practically all the large and respectable outlets will be barred to me. If so, I shall just have to keep writing more articles and books than ever!

So it has gone; and so, by and large, do I expect it to go in the future. Sex frankness breeds sex suppression. This, I dare say, will not stop me from continuing to say and to write sex views and facts that should assuredly be said and written. But—to be utterly realistic—it will definitely curb and limit me in this connection.

This is too bad; but not, fortunately, fatal.

8.

How Males Contribute to Female Frigidity

Most female frigidity that I have seen in my clinical practice has been either directly or indirectly caused by male ideas and practices.

Much of the so-called frigidity I hear about, in fact, turns out to be nothing of the sort: since many women who come to complain that they are sexually anesthetic turn out to be, on closer questioning, fully as capable of orgasm as are their male consorts—and frequently much more so. But their *notions* of their sex capacities are so distorted and warped that they imagine an in-

114

competence that they do not truly possess; and these female notions are almost always derived from similar nonsensical ideas believed in and propagated by presumably sophisticated males.

In our society, males cause and abet female frigidity —or, actually, pseudofrigidity—in several major ways. The first of these is by constructing a theory of female orgasm that, while neatly designed to bolster the male ego, has little or nothing to do with the facts of female anatomy.

Thus, psychologists like Sigmund Freud (1924–1950), reasoning that young girls masturbate by manipulating their external sex organs (particularly the clitoris) and that older women often obtain a climax through having sexual intercourse, have concluded that the normal woman *should* be satisfied through having coitus, and that if she is not she is sexually immature or neurotic.

And physiologists and physicians, such as Dr. Arnold Kegel (1952, 1956), have concluded that since women have vaginal contractions in the course of their orgasms, and that since certain muscles are involved in setting off these contractions, the normal woman *should* have well-developed vaginal muscles, and penile stimulation of these muscles, in order to have a "complete" or "full" orgasm.

These theories are all very interesting and seemingly logical. The trouble is that, in the case of literally millions of women, they simply do not work.

For curiously enough, in spite of all the male hullabaloo about how females *should* have so-called vaginal orgasms in order to be sexually "mature" or "fulfilled," the fact remains that many women, in the course of their entire lives, rarely or never *do* experience this kind of climax.

Yet there can be no doubt that many—perhaps most —of these vaginally frigid women not only obtain perfectly satisfactory orgasms all their lives, but regularly obtain more frequent, more intense, and more lasting peaks of sex satisfaction than do the majority of males (the Hegelers, 1963; Kelly, 1953; Kinsey et al., 1953; the Kronhausens, 1964; Masters and Johnson, 1961, 1962).

Why, then, the male emphasis in our culture on the *right* way that a female *should* obtain orgasm? Jealousy of women's greater prowess in this area? Perhaps. Unwillingness to accord women true equality of sexual status? Possibly. More to the point, however, seems to be an even simpler explanation: namely, that because the *male* is very nicely satisfied with vaginal intromission, or coitus, he thinks that it is only cricket that the female should *also* be. And when, as is often true, she is not, but turns out to possess another organ of satisfaction, the clitoris, which affords *him*, the male, relatively little satisfaction, he simply cannot bring himself to understand *why* this should be.

So he quickly dreams up, and dogmatically writes up in textbooks, theories which conclusively "prove" that any woman who, unlike most men, does not specifically enjoy and have a terrific orgasm in the course of vaginal copulation—that woman is unquestionably

116

"immature," "peculiar," or "disturbed." The sorriest part of this game is that when these obviously male-centered and defensively hewn ideas become sufficiently repeated and endlessly quoted they soon take on the aura no longer of speculative theory but of indubitable fact (Bergler, 1961; Robinson, 1962; Reich, 1961).

As a result, not only males but virtually all females start to believe their never-proven "validity," and many of these females become so disturbed by not having their climaxes as they are theoretically *supposed* to have them that some finally throttle them completely and become incapable of obtaining either vaginal or extravaginal intense sensations. Their consequent frigidity is then taken as evidence in proof of the original hypothesis that they are just neurotic women!

The core of considerable female frigidity in our society, then, is the masculine attitude that because males are easily satisfied in coitus, females should *also* be. This leads to an almost automatic corollary: namely, that males who believe this theory invariably have poor sexual technique. At the very best, they are aware of several copulative or non-copulative variations which result in fairly rapid satisfaction for themselves; at the worst, they insist on one quick, preliminaryless form of intercourse (usually with the male surmounting the female in the face to face position), and that is that.

In either event, these coitus-fixated males rarely recognize the female need for preliminary love-making, including extravaginal and vaginal stimulation with other parts of their anatomy than their sacred penises. And in those rare instances where they do attempt nonpenile contacts with their female consorts, they are invariably shocked by the notion that these contacts should often, and with some women always, be continued up to and including the woman's climax (Ellis, 1960; 1963a; 1963b; 1963c; 1963d).

In other words: when the males of our society finally are forced to acknowledge that there is nothing sacred about intercourse, and that there are several *other* legitimate means of heterosexual satisfaction, they still, for the most part, insist on looking at nonpenile and nonvaginal contacts as necessarily *preliminary* ones—preliminary, of course, to coitus. The fact that extracoital contacts may, in, of, and by themselves, be completely fulfilling and rewarding—this obvious fact of human sex anatomy and physiology is generally relegated to oblivion, or, if considered at all, put under the rubric of "perversion" or "abnormality."

Actually, as I will show elsewhere in this book, sexual perversion does *not* consist of an individual's having noncoital sex acts, but consists of his having *any* kind of sexual participation, including coitus, on an exclusive, fixated, or fetishistic basis.

To round out the business of frigidicizing females in our culture, many males are perfectly aware that their female partners cannot and should not be satisfied only through intercourse; and they know full well that noncoital sex techniques, where indulged on a non-fetishistic basis, are not correctly to be labeled "perversions" or "abnormalities."

Still, because they do not want to take the relatively little time and trouble necessary to satisfy their mates in extra-coital ways, they consistently refuse to do so. Yet, these same men tend to be horribly shocked when their wives do not have dinner ready on time, or neglect mending their socks, or forget to get the laundry done by the time they need a clean shirt. And although they act enormously grieved when their wives would like them to cooperate in helping them achieve orgasms, woe betide these same wives if they are vaginally unreceptive when these males decide that their abstinence of the last two days has gone much too far!

Because, then, myriads of men in our society insist that women *should* be sexually satisfied solely through coitus; because these men frequently make very poor lovers; and because they are often quite sexually selfish themselves while expecting their wives to be fully receptive whenever the spirit moves these males. for these reasons do we have millions of women who, in spite of their having perfectly wonderful capacities for sex satisfaction, actually are quite anesthetic or frigid.

Statistical proof of this sorry state of affairs may be found in the works of Katherine Davis (1929), Dickinson and Beam (1931), G. V. Hamilton (1929), Lewis M. Terman (1938, 1951), Alfred C. Kinsey (1953), and

119

other investigators of our sex behavior. Even more convincing clinical proof may be found in clinical practice.

In my own psychological practice, I find many women who come for help largely because they consider themselves frigid and who discover, after I have seen them (and often their husbands) for a few weeks or months, that their sexual capacities easily exceed that of the average male. One thirty-year-old woman, who had been married for ten years, came because her husband kept complaining that she did not enjoy sex relations and did not seem to obtain any orgasm. After considerable questioning, I determined that she usually did achieve a climax in sex relations, but that it was so slight and inconsequential that she hardly knew that she was having one.

Further questioning elicited the fact that this woman was so petrified by her husband's demands that she derive great satisfaction from intercourse that she actually derived little or no satisfaction from it. My dialogue with her proceeded in this manner:

Therapist: So every time you have intercourse with your husband, you are worried about how you are going to behave during it, about how you are going to react to it—is this correct?

Client: Yes. I keep wondering whether or not I'll have a climax, and whether he will be pleased.

Therapist: But that's exactly the thing to make sure that you will *not* have an orgasm!

Client: You mean that I block myself in this manner?

120

Therapist: That's just what I mean. *Anyone* who does *anything* in this manner tends to block herself from doing it adequately or well. Anyone who worries about *how* she is doing, instead of concentrating on *what* she is doing, inevitably diverts herself from the real problem at hand and performs poorly.

Client: Why is that?

Therapist: It's a simple matter of diversion, or lack of proper focusing. The human brain, somewhat like a calculating machine, actually seems to concentrate well on only one thing at a time. Even when you listen to music and read, you are usually not doing either act particularly well, but are wavering somewhat between the music and the reading matter. Isn't that so?

Client: Well, uh, I think I see what you mean. When I listen to music, really listen to it that is, I often can read a whole page without knowing what is on it. And when I concentrate on the reading, I hardly know what music is playing.

Therapist: Exactly. Well, other human performances, including sexual ones, are just like that. If you concentrate or focus clearly on A, you can't focus too well on B; and *vice versa*.

Client: So if I concentrate on what my husband is thinking about my sexual performance, I can't, at the same time, focus too well on actually performing—is that it?

Therapist: That's just it. As long as you worry about how well you're doing sexually—which really means how well you're doing in your husband's eyes—you will find it impossible to think about what you are doing—which should be, of course, enjoying yourself.

Client: But what about my husband?

Therapist: Well, what about him?

Client: I—I mean, uh, what about his pleasure? What about his wanting me to have an orgasm?

Therapist: That, I am afraid, is *his* problem. Naturally, he will find it more satisfying, in many instances, if you fully enjoy sex. And he should help you try to enjoy it. But is his harping on your getting an orgasm every time helping you in any way?

Client: No; quite the contrary.

Therapist: And is it helping *him*?

Client: No, I guess it isn't. He's just getting disgruntled and disappointed when I don't have a climax.

Therapist: All right, then: his harping on, or worrying too much about, *your* orgasm isn't helping you and isn't helping him. Obviously, then, he'd do better to stop this senseless worry, and it is his problem if he doesn't. By all means, let him get help, then, with his problem.

Client: But shouldn't he want me to have satisfaction?

Therapist: Yes, he should *want* it—but not *require* it. He should prefer your having a terrific sex climax, but not have a *dire need* of your having one. After all, if you don't have one, it's mainly your loss, isn't it, rather than his?

Client: Yes, but what of his ego?

Therapist: Ego? You mean, don't you, his *lack of ego?* If he had true ego-strength, or self-confidence, he wouldn't *need* to keep bolstering it by showing himself how good he was at giving you sex pleasure. But because he doesn't like himself well enough, doesn't have enough confidence in his *own* self, he has to keep proving to himself how "good" he is by showing what power he has to give *you* an orgasm. What kind of strength is that?

Client: Not very good, I guess.

Therapist: No, not very good at all. But that, as I say, is his problem, and he should get help with it. If he wants to talk to me about it, I'll be glad to talk to him; otherwise, he can see some other competent therapist. But let's get back to *your* problem.

Client: Yes, let's.

Therapist: Your problem is not, really, what your husband thinks about your having an orgasm but what *you* think about his thinking about your having it.

Client: I didn't quite get that.

Therapist: Let me repeat: Your problem, like anyone's problem, is practically never what another human being thinks or does, but what *you* think about what he thinks or does.

Client: So if I don't care too much about what another, about what my husband, thinks or does, then I don't have a problem?

Therapist: That's right. At least, you don't have a neurotic problem; but you may have the original problem in its own right. Take your so-called frigidity, for example. If you don't care too much, worry too much about your husband's attitude toward it, you will not

123

be needlessly or illogically concerned—or what we normally call neurotic. *Then,* when you have overcome your neurosis in this connection, you can go back to considering the *real* problem—which, as I said before, is simply that of how *you* can enjoy yourself sexually.

Client: And you think I can solve that problem, that real problem, if I stop concentrating on the false problem, the one my husband is creating by his worrying about my having an orgasm?

Therapist: I am sure that you can. If you stop worrying about his worries, and mainly concentrate when you have sex relations, on your own sex feelings, on what excites and satisfies you, then you will find it almost impossible *not* to have much more gratification than you are now having.

This client did, thereafter, concentrate on her own sex pleasures when she was having relations with her husband, and within a few more weeks she was getting stronger and stronger reactions. Two months after she first came for therapy, she was not only having intense climaxes most of the time she had intercourse, but was also having three or four terrific climaxes a night—while her husband, quite amazed, could not keep up with her, and had to resort to extracoital methods of satisfying her on most occasions.

This, then, is what I often find clinically, but what I would be far more pleased, in the future, *not* to keep finding—if only the males in our culture would stop contributing to female frigidity, and if only our females would stop taking them, in this respect, too seriously.

9.

Sexual Inadequacy in the Male

What the exact figures on male sexual inadequacy are no one, at present, knows. But judging from all existing indications, the chances are that they are enormous. My own estimate, from detailed questioning of many hundreds of male and female clients and friends, is that probably three out of four American men are much less sexually competent than they theoretically could be.

Sexual inadequacy in the male takes several main forms: (1) general lack of desire; (2) reaching a climax too rapidly (premature ejaculation); (3) inability to maintain an erection; (4) inability to achieve a climax at all; and (5) general inhibition, leading to the inability to enjoy sex relations fully or to satisfy the female partner.

According to most psychological and sexological texts, these kinds of male inadequacy are rarely based on physical deficiencies but are rooted in the individual's emotional disturbances. This, in general, is true: although it must be acknowledged that physical causes, such as glandular imbalances, disease processes, and general physical disability, play an important part in some sexual malfunctionings (Caprio, 1960; Hirsch, 1961, 1962).

It is also true, as the textbooks say, that some cases of sexual impotence and anesthesia are the result of deepseated, long-standing neurotic tendencies on the part of the male, including unresolved Oedipal feeling, underlying hostility against women, unconscious hatred of his particular female partner, and so on.

Nonetheless, I have found in clinical practice that most sex disabilities in men take a generalized rather than a highly specialized neurotic pattern and that this pattern does not differ significantly from the pattern of nonsexual disturbance which so many members of our populace, male and female, acquire. More specifically: I find that most cases of male inadequacy are caused by a general fear-of-failure pattern of behavior rather than by some special sex problem (Ellis, 1962a).

The fear-of-failure pattern works along the following

lines: (1) The individual feels that he *should* be good at some activity, such as sexual intercourse. (2) He fears that he will *not* be good at it, and that this will be catastrophic (for example, the girl he fails to satisfy will hate him and think him an idiot). (3) Because of his fears, and because of the fact that all humans fail in certain activities from time to time, he experiences actual failure on a few occasions. (4) This convinces him that he really is incompetent at the desired activity. (5) He then begins to become more and more anxious about his performance; and, because of his anxiety, to perform less and less well. (6) A terrible vicious circle is thereby established: fear of failure leads to actual failure which in turn leads to more fear of failure.

Add to this fear-of-failure pattern the fact that, in contemporary America, sex is one of the least openly, most hedged-in activities practiced, and the result is a general holocaust.

For if you are afraid to fail at anything—let us say, for example, swimming—the best way to get over your fear is to keep practicing the thing you fear—to swim and swim and swim. But how can one who is afraid of sex failure practice sex activity, when, both premaritally and postmaritally, he is most likely to be hemmed in with every possible kind of self-imposed, partner-imposed, and society-imposed restriction? How can he, with our terrific sex tabus, even honestly face the fact that he has a sex problem—as, say, he would face the fact that he had a swimming problem?

SEX WITHOUT GUILT

At every turn, the individual in our culture who is
sexually inadequate and who wants to overcome his
inadequacy runs smack up against social restrictions
and pressures.

How so? In these ways:

The sexually inadequate male, in order to get over
his fear of failure, should first of all rid himself of the
idea that the one "proper" and "normal" way of satisfying a female sexually is literally by coitus. As is pointed
out in another section of this book, females are frequently not satisfiable by sexual intercourse alone; and
even when they are, it is a rare male who can satisfy the
fully healthy, sexually released woman coitally, for the
good reason that whereas the average man is capable of
having intercourse several times a week, innumerable
women are capable of having it several times a day. The
male who exclusively relies on his penis, therefore, to
fulfill the sex needs of a moderately sexed woman, is
often doomed to failure at the start. Yet, in our society,
if he starts thinking, as he theoretically should, of noncoital means of satisfying his partner, he runs against
age-old superstitions and blockings.

Secondly, the sexually inadequate male who wants
to better his lot should begin to look upon some failures
as normal and to accept the fact that none of us are
as young as we once were, and that a man in his thirties
or forties cannot be expected to maintain the sexual
peaks of a boy in his teens.

Here he runs smack against the general competitive
mores of our culture, which loudly, if quite falsely, pro-

claim that everyone should be better than everyone else at everything he does, and that everyone should always better his own previous performance. With competitive philosophies like this being ceaselessly drummed into his head, our sexually incompetent male can hardly help making himself increasingly fearful and incompetent.

Thirdly, the male who is beginning to have some difficulties should learn to control his thinking while he is having sex relations. If he suffers from premature ejaculation, he should learn to think of sexually non-exciting things while having intercourse; and if he suffers from inability to maintain an erection or achieve an orgasm, he should learn to think of sexually arousing images and to try variations which are particularly exciting to him.

Here our societal sex tabus again rise up to smite down the would-be adequate male: since he is usually taught that some of the sex acts which he should think about or execute to maintain his best performance are "immoral" or "perverted" or "abnormal." And, believing this nonsense, he refuses to let himself go sexually—and consequently remains inadequate.

Fourthly, as previously noted, the best way to eliminate any fear is to do the thing you fear over and over: to gain more and more practice at it. But, in our society, for a sexually incompetent individual to keep having steady sex relations is often the most difficult thing in the world.

If he is unmarried, we make his sex practicing quite

difficult to achieve; and if he is married, we make it depend almost entirely on the good-will and lack of disturbance of his wife. In either event, what generally happens is that the not too adequate male finally becomes, from lack of experience, still more inadequate.

Finally, male inadequacy can be overcome if the relatively incompetent male gets over his general sex inhibitions, throws himself fully into the sex acts he performs, and shows his partner that he believes sex is a fine and wonderful thing for both of them and that they should make every effort to enjoy it to the utmost.

This, more specifically, involves the male's frankly talking with his partner about their sex proclivities and needs, candidly discussing the times when they fail, and openly planning better procedures for their next participation. But this kind of verbal and active uninhibitedness, again, is definitely discouraged in our antisexual culture, and can only be achieved by those who stalwartly defy this culture, to some extent, rather than those who completely conform to it.

Summing up: most male sexual inadequacy in our society is caused not so much by deepseated, particularized psychological disturbances as by a more generalized fear of failure, on the one hand, and sexual puritanism, on the other hand. Then, when the individual becomes embroiled in a terrible vicious circle of fear of failure inciting to actual failure which in turn produces further fear, he has tremendous difficulty overcoming his increasing sexual inadequacy. Because society, once again, sets up barriers of competitiveness and antisexuality which make it almost impossible for him to do anything about his sexual incompetence. By *this* time, the individual is often so disturbed by his boxed-in and seemingly hopeless condition that he really does develop a full-blown neurosis.

The solution?

As usual, there is no perfect solution within the framework of the present social order (Ellis, 1965a). Certain individuals can distinctly be helped by going for psychotherapy—which, when it is effectively done, will help them adjust to the inadequacies of their culture by selectively accepting and ignoring certain of its dictates.

But most individuals will, by the very nature of their social upbringing, resist even airing their sex problems to professional therapists and will doggedly continue to "live" with these problems. To which, for the present, we can only say: alas.

131

10.

When Are We Going to Quit Stalling
About Sex Education?

More nonsense is written about sex education than about virtually any other popular subject. In spite of these writings, or perhaps in some measure because of them, American sex attitudes, as I have shown in my books *The Folklore of Sex* and *The American Sexual Tragedy,* are thoroughly confused.

Thus, we heartily believe in sex education—and do little or nothing about it.

132

We say that we should go all out to teach our children the facts of life—and then, in our sex education materials, delete most of the realistic facts from life.

We put on determined sex education campaigns—and then see that our young people are so abysmally ignorant that they undergo innumerable unwanted pregnancies, unnecessary abortions, forced marriages, gruesome wedding nights, terrible sex fears, and needless divorces.

The truth is that our sex education today is bound to be emasculated: for the simple reason that our *general* sex beliefs and feelings are inconsistent and muddled. Most of us are not even aware of our now-you-see-them-and-now-you-don't sex attitudes, as their deepest roots are unconscious rather than conscious. Typically, we seem to think one way about sex—and actually think quite another.

For example, we consciously are horrified by the thought of premarital sex relations and adultery—and we unconsciously envy, laugh with, and even applaud fornicators and adulterers. Or we consciously think abortion is permissible—and unconsciously castigate ourselves for taking any part in one.

When, with our many open and underlying sex conflicts, we try to teach our children the objective and scientific facts of sex, we inevitably fumble pretty badly. We want to be oh so casual and cool about conveying the facts of life; instead, we tend to stammer, blush, look out of the window, paw restlessly at the floor with our feet, or otherwise avoid coming to direct, matter-of-fact terms with the subject we are trying to present. But children, of course, sense our feelings as well as our words. And telling them that sex is a perfectly natural and beautiful part of life while you are hum-hawing to beat all get-out is like trying to persuade them that you love your mother-in-law while you are using her picture as a spit target.

Let's face it: good sex education needs good sex teachers—teachers who are themselves free from irrational taboos; who think that sex is good clean fun; who have had a fine and abundant sex life themselves; and who can handle their own sex problems in much the same manner as they solve nonsexual life situations.

These teachers, whether they be parents or professionals, should of course present sex education in a global, total-pattern manner, as part of a unified picture of life. Human sex behavior cannot be divorced from emotion, personality, social living, economic affairs, and the other complex aspects of modern living. These teachers should not, under the guise of placing the facts of sex in the general context of life, instill irrelevant, guilt-producing notions that will deluge sexual science under a pietistic landslide.

No one, for example, would begin to teach a child homemaking tasks and responsibilities by beginning: "The home is a sacred place, and cooking and cleaning are beautiful God-given occupations which must always be carried out in a serious and sober manner, so that the fundamental purposes of life may be gloriously fulfilled." Yet, this is the kind of hokum with which our books and talks on sex education are commonly filled.

Naturally, when handed this type of "enlightenment," the bright child quickly begins to wonder what it is about sex that is so intrinsically filthy that mealy-mouthed words by the dozen are needed to help clean it up.

Once again: our children are virtually never taught that playing baseball is a worthy pastime—but that you must not talk about it publicly. Or that reading is an estimable occupation—but that *book, hero,* and *read* are nasty four-letter words which you must never say aloud. Or that playing chess is a wonderful sport— providing that you do not play it with your mother, father, sister, brother, other blood relations, any member of your own sex, and all but one single member of the other sex in your entire lifetime. Yet, while smugly assuring our youngsters that coitus is the finest and most beautiful thing in the world, we seriously caution them not to engage in, speak about, or ever privately think about it—except, perhaps, on any Fourth of July that happens to fall on Monday of a leap year. And then we wonder why, as adolescents and adults, they happen to have numberless sex problems!

What, then, is the answer?

Very frankly, as I point out in *The Case for Sexual Liberty* (1965a), there is no perfect, or even half-perfect, answer. Societal sex attitudes must be changed as a *whole* before we can reasonably expect *individual* sex education to be truly effective.

If you, for example, managed to surmount your own

135

sex biases to some extent, and to present your child with objective, scientific sex viewpoints, you would be producing a youngster who would largely be out of step with his own community: since it is most unlikely that many of the other parents in your region would have given their children a similarly objective sexual frame of reference. The result would be that your youngster, while he might well be less sexually disturbed than his peers, would still tend to suffer from the disturbances of his environment: which is a sorry, and yet none the less incontrovertible, fact to contemplate.

Is the case of sex education in present-day America entirely hopeless then? No, not entirely. On the practical side, there are still a few things you can do to help along the cause of honest-to-goodness sex education in this and succeeding generations. Here are some suggestions:

1. Recognize your own sex ignorance and limitations and do not pretend that you know what you obviously do not know about sex and love.

2. Read as many scientific and factual books and articles on the subject as you can—and read everything that you do read most critically. Ignore all opinions that are moralistic or sectarian and try to draw conclusions from data rather than dogma.

3. Face your own sex problems squarely and honestly—and run, do not walk, to the nearest psychologist or marriage counselor when you are sexually disturbed.

4. As soon as your children begin asking sex ques-

tions, answer them in a direct, factual, down-to-earth manner. Teach them that sex, in virtually all its aspects, is a fine, pleasurable thing. But also teach them, prophylactically, that the world is presently full of bigots and ignoramuses who think otherwise and who will try to make them feel guilty about their sexuality. Tell them that, unfortunately, they will often have to obey against public display of nudity—but that as long as the laws and mores of these bigots—such as the laws they are discreet, they can, in the privacy of their own thoughts and boudoirs, guiltlessly keep their own counsels.

5. If you have any qualms about giving proper sex education to your children, do not hesitate to call on other qualified persons to help you do so. Psychologists, physicians, marriage counselors, teachers, and others who have specialized in sex education will be glad to be of service in this connection.

6. Above all, try to be as accepting, non-critical, and democratic about the sex behavior of others as you can possibly be. Take the same attitudes toward sex ethics and morals as you would toward general ethics and morals. Work, in whatever way you can, for rules and laws which seek only to discourage sex acts whereby one individual needlessly, gratuitously, and distinctly harms another being, rather than statutes and mores which are based on supersitition, ignorance, and sadistic sex "morality."

11.

How American Women Are Driving American Males Into Homosexuality

Although the American female population between the ages of 20 and 40 only slightly outnumbers the male population, our females are always complaining that it is very difficult for them to find eligible males. And they are probably right.

In addition to the large numbers of males who are taken out of circulation because they are in military service, in prison, in out of the way places, or otherwise inaccessible, there are millions of others who are theo-

138

retically available for feminine companionship, but who are actually self-removed from any possibility of satisfying heterosexual relations. These are our exclusive or nearly-exclusive homosexuals.

Dr. Alfred C. Kinsey (1948, 1953) and his associates estimate that of the two or three million Americans who, for long periods of their life, are completely uninterested in heterosexual relations, about three-fourths are males and only one-fourth females. Donald Webster Cory, author of the authoritative book, *The Homosexual in America* (1963), feels that "the homosexual males outnumber the lesbians by about three or four to one . . . Some of my homosexual friends assert that the males outnumber the females by as much as ten to one." My own observations based on many years of sex research and clinical practice, lead me to believe that American confirmed homosexual males outnumber their lesbian sisters by at least five to one.

The grim irony is that the women of our culture, who suffer most by this discrepancy between homosexuals and lesbians, are in many ways directly responsible for the existence of so much homosexuality. For, as psychological and psychoanalytic authors have been pointing out for many years now, women are the chief child-raisers of our society, and in the rearing of their sons they often encourage the development of homosexuality. Thus, mothers often tie their sons so closely to them that these sons cannot possibly become emotionally or sexually interested in other women, and hence are driven to seek male sex companionship.

They raise their male offspring in such a puritanical fashion that any heterosexual desires or actions on their part would cause them to be powerfully guilty and frequently sexually impotent.

They sometimes, feeling more comfortable themselves with female rather than male children, raise their sons in a distinctly feminine manner and consciously or unconsciously encourage these sons to adopt a feminine role in life.

They frequently instill in their sons such high and unrealistic ideals of "manliness" that these sons become morbidly afraid to fail in their "masculine" roles, and consequently run away from "manly" responsibilities into the easier paths of homosexuality (Ellis, 1963d, 1965b; Bieber et al., 1962).

In many ways, then, as the psychological texts tell us, American women keep raising American men to turn to homosexuality. What these texts rarely explain, however, is the role of young women—the very women, that is, who are so desirous these days of gaining male companionship and, ultimately, marriage—in driving our men to seek sex satisfaction with other men.

This role may best be epitomized in the words of Donald, one of my very bright and goodlooking respondents in a study of "normal" homosexuals that I made. Donald once had a quite satisfactory relationship with a college-level girl from one of America's finest families who wanted him enough to be sexually aggressive; but after breaking up with her, had returned to exclusive homosexuality. I asked him why he did not continue

140

going with girls. His answer was something of a shocker:

"Why," asked Donald, "should I bother with girls when I can so easily get men who satisfy me? All I have to do to get a fellow is to go in to any gay bar and, after an hour or so at most, I invariably find some boy to go home with who will be very good sexually. Suppose, now, I want to find a girl instead of a boy. Where, to begin with, can I meet one without going through all sorts of trouble to get friends to introduce me and things like that? Then, suppose I do meet a girl and I think she's all right. I have to dress up, call for her at her home, take her out, probably spend a good deal of money on her, and do all sorts of things I may not want to do. And at the end of all that, I still don't really have her, and the chances are I'll have to keep seeing her several times before I can even get to do any heavy petting with her. Hell, it's not worth it! And if I do get anywhere with her, she right away wants to marry me, even though we really have little in common. I'm sure I could have just as much pleasure with a girl as I do with a boy. But there's too much trouble attached to getting it."

Is Donald typical of many other homosexuals? Alas, yes. I have in my files of patients and research cases many Donalds who have been discouraged from going with girls and have been literally driven or encouraged to become or to remain homosexual because the females whom they dated were callous, captious, and cautious, and who were interested in every kind of heterosexual

141

relations *except* actual sex contact. And since these males were—as, let us be candid, males generally are—*primarily* interested in sex affairs, they soon learned that they could more logically find such contacts in the homosexual than in the heterosexual world (Cory and Leroy, 1963; Stearn, 1963).

This is not to state or in any way imply that American females are to *blame* for the current mixed up state of affairs that is relentlessly driving millions of our males into homosexuality. The females, after all, are raised in our general culture, of which both sexes are an integral part, and which our males do just as much, and often more, to perpetuate as do our females.

The hard fact remains, however, that as a result of this culture, females, who are particularly reared to desire male companionship, are now frequently acting in such a sexual (or, rather, nonsexual) manner as to impel hordes of males to desert them for sex contacts with other males. And then these females are complaining bitterly about the dearth of eligible masculine courters.

The solution?

Theoretically only two workable solutions would seem to be available. Either (a) we must rear our males to be less interested in sex and more interested in the nonsexual aspects of heterosexual relations or (b) we must raise our females to be more interested in premarital relations of a heterosexual nature.

Both these possible solutions are most difficult to apply. If we try to induce the males in our culture to be less interested in sex and more concerned with the amative aspects of heterosexual relations, we immediately run into a biosocial block. The fact remains that young males are usually driven to some kind of orgasmic release and that, for their physical satisfaction as well as their growth and development as human beings, it is far better that they have their sex release with females than in most other outlets.

The idea that the human male can easily sublimate his sex desires into other more "idealistic" channels is largely nonsense that is not supported by any factual evidence. All the evidence we do have, as originally shown in Dr. William S. Taylor's famous monograph, *A Critique of Sublimation in Males* (1933), indicates that healthy young men can forego one kind of sex activity—such as coitus—for another kind of sex act—such as masturbation or homosexual behavior—but that that is just about as far as their ability to sublimate normally goes. Recommending that, instead of having sex outlets, these young males should take hot baths, run around the block, or become amorously but not sexually devoted to girls simply won't work—or will only work for a few rather abnormal males. It is just as realistic to advocate that virile young men should substitute romantic love for sex as it is to ask hungry youngsters to read the classics instead of eating.

The other logical solution to the problem of reducing male homosexuality, that of raising our females so that they are more interested in premarital relations of a heterosexual nature, is theoretically an excellent one;

but it is not likely to be put into practice in the near future because of our longstanding social restrictions and prejudices regarding prenuptial affairs. Such affairs, as we note in Chapter 3, have distinct advantages as well as disadvantages. They are also, if clinical and research observations are reliable, becoming more frequent on the part of unmarried females. But the likelihood is not too high that, in the next few decades, premarital relations in our society will become so routine as to make homosexual participations much less inviting than they now often are.

This means, in effect, that most probably nothing will be done to change the existing state of sexual affairs in this country—and that, in consequence, American women will continue to drive literally millions of men into homosexuality. And that the cries of some of the worst victims of this state of affairs—the females who perpetuate it—will continue to resound lamentably through the land.

12.

Another Look at Sexual Abnormality

Some few years ago I published a paper, which is re-printed in my book, *The Psychology of Sex Offenders*, in which I contended that we have no absolute criterion of what is sexual "normality"; and, in fact, "normal" sex behavior is anything and everything which we—or which the societies in which we happen to live —declare and make it to be.

Sex "normality," I said, is a relative, culturally con-ditioned phenomenon, and *no* mode of sex behavior is absolutely, finally, and for all times and places "normal"

145

or "abnormal." Groups which *think* various types of sex behavior "abnormal" automatically tend to *make* them so.

At the same time, I have also written several papers and books in which I insist that any individual who can *only*, under *all* circumstances, enjoy one particular form of sexual activity; anyone who is compulsively or obsessively fixated on one single mode of sexual behavior; anyone who is fearfully and rigidly bound to any *exclusive* form of sexual participation; that individual is unquestionably sexually abnormal, perverted, or neurotic (Ellis, 1960, 1963c, 1963d).

Is there any essential contradiction between these two publicly expressed views? I think not.

Consider, first, my contention that anyone who *exclusively* and *compulsively* engages in one form of sexual activity—such as, for example, homosexuality—is clearly acting in an illogical, irrational, childish, fixated, fetishistic, inflexible, and rigid manner and is therefore abnormal or neurotic.

In spite of the shocked emotionalism of many homosexuals and heterosexuals who have reacted violently against this statement, it still seems to me scientifically incontrovertible. For if we extend the proposition to nonsexual areas, it immediately becomes acceptable to virtually all those who cannot accept it in sexual realms.

Thus, as I point out in my book, *The American Sexual Tragedy*, an individual who is in good physical health and has no special allergic reactions, who insists on eating *nothing but* meat and potatoes; or who *only* will eat at three in the morning and will not touch a bit of food at any other time, even if he is starving; or who can eat *exclusively* on a set of blue plates and will absolutely refuse to eat on plates of any other color—such an individual, as almost anyone will acknowledge, is obviously abnormal, neurotic, or, in common parlance, crazy. Why, then, should not sexually fixated or obsessed individuals be similarly viewed?

From a purely biological standpoint, man is a plurisexual animal who has at least five major modes of obtaining sexual satisfaction. He may reach a sexual climax through (a) nocturnal emissions or waking thoughts; (b) masturbation; (c) heterosexual relations; (d) homosexual relations; and (e) sex relations with animals. Moreover, under each of these major modes of sex satisfaction exist almost countless sub-methods or variations. The chances are therefore, if any man or woman were raised on a desert island, without any specific sex teachings or prejudices, he or she would engage, at different times, in all the major and many of the minor modes of achieving a sex climax.

We are not so raised, however; and, consequently, we normally are prejudiced against engaging in certain sex acts, such as bestiality, and limit our sex activities to relatively few others. Nonetheless, even in our anti-sexual society, we are given considerable leeway in this connection, so that most of us, before we die, engage in, at the very least, masturbation, nocturnal emissions and several modes of heterosexual activities.

147

SEX WITHOUT GUILT

The relatively few of us who allow ourselves *no* leeway in this respect, but who are instead fixated on one *single* mode of sex behavior—such as, for instance, *only* having sexual intercourse and *no* other mode of activity (e.g., petting) with our wives—tend to be, in my opinion, distinctly neurotic or abnormal.

Moreover, those of us who under *no* circumstances— for example, if they were imprisoned with members of their own sex for thirty years—would consider foregoing their usual heterosexual activities for masturbatory or homosexual ones: these individuals, too, are in my estimation distinctly sexually fixated, abnormal, and neurotic. For such overly-rigid individuals are obviously being *exclusively* oriented toward one mode of sex activity not because they happen to prefer it, or have been strongly conditioned toward it, but because they are illogically and childishly *afraid* of trying any other mode of sex relations. It is this irrationality, this fear on their part which constitutes their sexual deviation or neurosis.

By the same token, our common Greenwich Village-type homosexuals are sexually abnormal or deviated not because they engage in sex relations with other males (which are biologically normal enough) but because they do so *exclusively*; because they are (consciously or unconsciously) *afraid* to try heterosexual outlets; because they are often disgusted by the mere thought of boy-girl relations; because they tend to be impotent in heterosexual affairs; and because they remain *compulsively* and *fixatedly* homosexual.

148

ANOTHER LOOK AT SEXUAL ABNORMALITY

Are we to conclude, then, that the only individual in our society who is perfectly normal sexually is one who actually engages in *all* kinds of activity, including heterosexual, homosexual, and animal relations? Naturally not: any more than we would not contend that anyone who did not eat all kinds of food would be abnormal.

A *reasonable* restriction or constriction of one's sex appetites is only to be expected—especially in a culture such as ours, which actively propagandizes against certain sex acts. I still insist, however, that when an individual in our society *completely*, under *all* circumstances, restricts himself to one and only one, form of sex outlet, then he is sexually abnormal or neurotic.

If the one mode of sex behavior to which he rigidly, under all circumstances, adheres is a very broad one, as well as one which is socially approved in our culture —such as heterosexual activity in general, including many of its sub-modes—then he is relatively little deviated or neurotic. If the one mode of sex behavior to which he rigidly adheres is a very narrow one, as well as one which is socially punishable in our culture— such as sex relations with sheep or homosexual relations of an exclusively anal nature—then he is relatively severely deviated or neurotic.

Sexual deviation or neurosis, therefore, exactly like nonsexual abnormality or neurosis, depends largely on the concepts of illogical, irrational, childish, fixated, fetishistic, inflexible, rigid, or exclusive behavior. And it relates not merely to an individual's *practicing* such

149

exclusive sex behavior, since at times he may practically be forced to do so (e.g., he may be exclusively homosexual because there are no women available); but to his *voluntarily continuing* to practice this exclusive behavior even when alternative modes are freely available or when he would have to be abstinent if he did not practice other modes.

A sex deviant or neurotic, in other words, *chooses* to remain fixated on one particular kind of sex activity because he would become illogically anxious or guilty if he did not do so.

How, then, does society *make* certain kinds of sex behavior "abnormal"? In several ways: (1) It arbitrarily bans some sex acts, such as homosexuality, and thereby encourages some individuals to become rebelliously fixated on these acts just *because* they are banned while it concomitantly encourages other individuals to become fearfully fixated on other sex acts which are not legally banned. (2) It raises many individuals to become exceptionally guilty about having certain sex desires—for example, the desire to have intercourse with underage girls—and, just because they are guilty, often become obsessed with precisely the desire about which they are guilty. (3) It teaches some persons to be anxious about their sexual capabilities; and, because of their anxiety, to withdraw from one sex area (e.g., heterosexuality) into another one (e.g., masturbation or homosexuality). (4) It raises numberless individuals with various complexes, such as the famous Oedipus and castration complexes, so that they feel uncomfortable maintaining their own-sex roles and frequently gravitate to other-sex roles and homosexual activities (Ellis, 1965b).

In these and many similar ways, society makes rules and inculcates prejudices which, when foisted upon the human individual, frequently cause him to react with anxiety and guilt—which, in turn, induce him to become sexually (as well as nonsexually) fixated upon illogical, rigid, exclusive forms of sex behavior, and thereby to become deviant or neurotic.

In the last analysis, then, sexual "abnormality" or neurosis results from the interaction of the human individual with his society and cannot be scientifically evaluated apart from both an individual and a social setting.

13.

On the Myths About Love

Many myths about love are wittingly or unwittingly promulgated in our newspapers, magazines, radio and TV shows, films, novels, songs, and other mass media. Indeed because of the attitudes on romance generally assumed by these media, it may well be opined that they usually contain more poetry than truth.

In consequence, perhaps the vast majority of Americans experience a love life that is remarkable for its meagerness and miserableness. Even their most significant amours tend to be so joyless and shallow that they add relatively little to the enhancement of living.

Some of the myths about love which are most prevalent in our culture will now be briefly examined.

1. *The myth that love is mysterious and that no one knows what it is.* Love, actually, is definable in quite simple terms. It is a human evaluation or emotion—and, like all emotion, a biased perception of something which causes one to react strongly to it in a favorable (or unfavorable) way.

Love arises when the individual evaluates something in a strong positive manner—that is, perceives it as being "good" or "beneficial" or "pleasant"—and moves toward or tries to possess it. Heterosexual love is a reasonably strong or intense attachment, involvement, or favorable prejudice between a male and a female. It usually, but not necessarily, includes passionate sex attraction between the lovers.

2. *The myth that there is such a thing as "real" or "true" love.* All love is true or real love in that it exists, and anything that exists is real. Love has three main vectors—frequency, intensity, and duration.

Many individuals, such as poets and novelists, have attempted to define "real" or "true" love in terms of intensity, and to contend that the only "true" love is a most intense, high-flown, once-in-a-lifetime feeling.

Many other individuals, such as clergymen, moralists, and social thinkers, have attempted to define "real" or "true" love in terms of duration, and to contend that the only "true" love is one that lasts for many years, and preferably forever.

Many psychologists have recently tried to define "true" love as one's interest in the growth and development of another person for *his* sake, rather than for one's *own* interest (Fromm, 1963).

Virtually no one has claimed that "true" love is frequently repeated, or often-entered love. Objectively viewed, however, "true" love exists only by some arbitrary definition, and all love, all emotional attachment, is actually true and real—simply because it exists.

3. *The myth that it is difficult to tell when one is in love.* Since love is simply a favorable bias or an emotional attachment from one person to another, it is very easy to tell when one is in love.

One loves whenever one feels, suspects, or imagines one is in love. One can also love unconsciously, without any realization that one loves; but most people who love have some definite inkling that they are favorably disposed toward another.

What is difficult to determine, in many instances, is not *that* one loves, but *how much* or *in what way* one loves, for there are almost infinite kinds and degrees of love. One may love sexually or non-sexually; mildly or passionately; heterosexually or homosexually; neurotically or normally; conjugally or non-conjugally; and so on.

Although *how* one loves is often, in itself, of little importance, it may become important if one contemplates doing something, such as marrying, because one loves.

4. *The myth that love and marriage always go together.* Marriage, in our society, is usually consummated today only if one loves, and presumably deeply loves, one's mate. In many other parts of the existing and historical world, that has not been true; and, even in our own society, marriage is still largely a socio-economic as well as an amative affair.

In a culture like our own, therefore, one probably should normally only marry an individual whom one loves; but, conversely, one should not by any means marry *everyone* one loves. One can theoretically love lots of people whom one meets within one's lifetime; but only a few of these, in all probability, would be suitable marital partners.

Moreover, if one open-eyedly wants to marry, or to stay married to, one whom one does not particularly love, that is certainly one's prerogative, and there is nothing intrinsically horrible about one's so doing. One *preferably* should marry, and remain married for love; but not *necessarily* (Ellis and Harper, 1961b).

5. *The myth that one can truly love only one person at a time.* There now exists a great mass of biographical and clinical evidence that shows that it is entirely possible for an individual to love, and to love in a deep, in-

155

tense manner, two or more members of the other sex at the same time.

This, in our society, normally leads to various complications. But the fact remains that exceptionally few individuals love only one member of the other sex for their entire lifetime; that many deeply love several times during their lives; and that in some of these instances they sincerely love two or more persons simultaneously.

Since most of us simultaneously love several of our close relatives, it is hardly surprising that we are capable of doing the same with two or more non-relatives. And since most of us tend to love that which we find lovable, it is highly unlikely that we will never find two lovable individuals on our horizon at one and the same time.

6. *The myth that when one loves one has no sex desires for individuals whom one doesn't love.* The human sex desires are deeply rooted in biological impulses and hormonally-based urges. They tend to be quite promiscuous and nondiscriminating in their own right. They are, in our culture, generally linked to the emotion of love, but there are many, many exceptions to the general rule.

Most individuals are sexually attracted to those members of the other sex whom they love; but they are also attracted to numerous members of the other sex for whom they have little or no love. It is therefore very common for an individual to love one member of the other sex very dearly, and to enjoy sex relations with this person, and yet to be highly sexually attracted to one or more other individuals. Indeed, the male or female in our culture who is *only* sexually attracted to his or her wife, and is *never* interested in any other member of the opposite sex, is a most unusual and, very probably, abnormal individual.

This does not mean that a married person has to *do* anything about his or her extramarital sex interests; but it is almost impossible not to have any such interests, even though one dearly loves one's mate.

7. *The myth that one loves one's beloved steadily or all the time.* Love, even when it is deepseated and intense, tends to be a distinctly intermittent rather than a steady, incessant feeling. This is especially true when one loves for any considerable length of time.

One steadily loves one's mate, in the sense that one may never think of divorcing her. But one does not steadily love her in the sense that one thinks of her incessantly and never has any neutral or negative feelings for her.

Indeed, the individual who was truly actively in love with his mate for twenty-four hours of every day in the year would be an exceptionally disturbed, obsessive individual, who would not be able to function effectively in the remaining aspects of his life. Such an individual would need psychotherapeutic treatment.

The average individual who loves, however, actively, violently, passionately loves for only a relatively few

157

minutes of each day; the rest of the time he tends to be rather neutral, and at times even antagonistic, to the beloved person.

These, then, are some of the most prevalent myths about love in our day. They are not only widely promulgated, but are unfortunately often believed. Hardly a day passes when some individual with pre-marital or marital difficulties does not walk into my office and present a problem which basically originates in and is sustained by one or more of these superstitions.

On the same working day, for example, I saw a young man who was terribly disturbed because, although en-gaged to and quite enamored of one girl, he had still been thinking sexually of other girls; and a woman who was exceptionally upset because her husband, who was quite kind to her and a good sex partner, kept show-ing friendly feelings toward other women as well.

Should, then, our means of mass communication be censored, and forbidden to publish myths about love which lead to so much heartache and emotional dis-turbance? Hell, no! But it might not be a bad idea, no, it might not be a bad idea at all, if large magazines, and film companies, and radio and TV networks, which spend so many millions of dollars buying romantic clap-trap for public consumption also spent a small part of those millions getting some professional advice on just how psychologically harmful is some of the material they produce.

Maybe if they had a good psychologist sit down with

some of their mushier authors, these authors might learn a few of the hard facts of life and their readers, listeners, and viewers might be considerably less likely to be traumatized with romantic twaddle.

14.

Sex Fascism

Although relatively few Americans could be legit-
imately labeled as political or economic fascists today,
probably the great majority are sex fascists. What is
perhaps even more surprising is that the sex fascists
tend, in some respects, to be just as prevalent among the
politico-economic liberal groups as they do among the
social bigots and reactionaries.

Sex fascism is a major subheading under what I call
intellectual fascism—which I find, among my clients
and my friends, to be perhaps the most pandemic and

virulent psychosocial disease of our times. So before I discuss sex fascism in particular, let me briefly say something about intellectual fascism in general.

Fascism, essentially, is the arbitrary belief that individuals who possess certain "desirable" traits are intrinsically superior to those who possess certain "undesirable" characteristics. Thus, people who are white, Aryan, or Christian are defined as being "good" or "worthwhile" and those who are Negro, non-Aryan, or Jewish are defined as being "inferior" or "worthless."

Intellectual fascism, instead of arbitrarily asserting that a certain set of physical traits is "superior" to another, capriciously points to a different group of human characteristics and dogmatically declares that *it* is "better" and that only individuals who possess *this* mark of distinction are truly worthwhile. The traits that are arbitrarily glorified by intellectual fascists are usually intelligence, culture, estheticness, achievement, success, etc. Where intellectual fascists often make a great to-do about how democratic they are in hobnobbing with Negroes or intermarrying with Jews or ignoring economic class distinctions in their friendships, the attitude they take toward anyone who is "stupid" or "incompetent" or "unartistic" is one of extreme condescension or scorn (Ellis, 1965c).

What intellectual fascists, exactly like politico-economic fascists, find it impossible to see is that their definitions of "superiority" and "worthwhileness" *are* arbitrary and definitional. "But intelligence and competence," they will insist, "definitely *are* better than

161

stupidity and incompetence. Why, then, should we not prefer a bright and capable person to a dull and incapable one?" In this insistence, they confuse several important issues:

First of all: such traits as intelligence and artistry, although good *for some purposes,* are not necessarily good *in themselves.* Thus, intelligence is fine for problem solving and artistry is most useful in decorating a home. But high intelligence may be a handicap in driving a truck or working at a monotonous job, and artistic sensitivity may be a disadvantage to someone who works in a coal mine or is stranded on a bleak desert island.

Second: politico-social fascists could argue, with equal logic, that a man's possessing blue eyes and blond hair gives him a more "esthetic" look than one who has brown eyes and black hair or that Aryans are superior to Jews because they suffer less frequently from certain diseases, such as diabetes. The fact that a given individual possesses *some* traits which are "better" or more advantageous than those possessed by others hardly makes him a *generally* superior being.

Third: a man's *preference* for a given characteristic should never be confused with the *intrinsic worth* of that characteristic. If I prefer twelve-toed or ivory-haired women above all others, that hardly proves that you and everyone else in the world has similar preferences. And even if the majority of us esteem twelve-toed women for, let us say, our wives or mistresses, that does not constitute valid evidence that ten-toed women are not good for *any other purpose,* nor that they cannot be worthwhile to themselves.

Fourth: assuming that the possession of certain characteristics may, under some or most circumstances, be preferable to the person who possesses these traits as well as to others, does this mean that those who are less fortunate, and who do not possess these traits, are utterly worthless, criminal, and ready for the ash can? Granting that tallness, or high intelligence, or physical strength may be useful for all or most humans to have, should those who are short, or of average intelligence, or unmuscular be induced to commit suicide or be led to the gas chambers?

Fifth: in the final analysis, any trait that is "good" or "superior" must be satisfactory or excellent for *something*—for some purpose. And that purpose must, to some extent, always be an arbitrary prejudice or judgment value. Thus, even a trait such as good health, which almost everyone accepts as being a "good" one, is only good for living, for leading an enjoyable life. But someone could question—as indeed many a someone already has questioned—the intrinsic value of life and enjoyment and could claim that it would be better if human living ceased. Consequently, *all* human characteristics are to some extent "good" only by arbitrary definition—good for some purpose which some individual or group has *stipulated* as being "beneficial" or "fine."

Intellectual fascists, then, exactly like politico-economic fascists, arbitrarily *define* certain human pur-

163

poses and traits as being "superior" and, in one way or another, they scorn, discriminate against, and put down those who do not possess these traits or strive for the favored purposes. Although they often claim to be super-democrats, they actually are exceptionally oligarchic or authoritarian in their basic beliefs of human value. What is more, where the political fascist mainly judges *others* by his arbitrary standards, and considers himself worthwhile for adhering to these standards and deems others worthless for not possessing the "elite" traits he demands, the intellectual fascist tends to judge himself as well as others by the perfectionistic esthetic-intellectual criteria he establishes, and to condemn himself, too, when he even temporarily fails to measure up to these ideals. He thus is in the unenviable position of being undemocratic and over-demanding toward everyone, including himself.

What has all this to do with sex fascism? Very much. For sex fascism is based on both politico-economic and intellectual fascism, and has some of the worst features of each.

First, let us consider the side of sex fascism that largely stems from the political authoritarianism of the Mussolini- and Hitler-type brands. One of the fundamental tenets of Nazism is that not only Jews and Negroes, but women as well, are second-class citizens whose main role should be that of catering to males and to the preservation of the race, rather than that of being personalities in their own right. This is what the sexual fascist believes too.

More specifically, the sexual fascist firmly upholds the double standard of sex morality. He thinks that women are radically different from men in their sexual desires; that they can invariably get along with less sex activity than males; that it is not too important if they do not achieve orgasm when they have sex relations; that when they do come to climax, they should be able to do so exactly as males do, in the course of coitus rather than in extracoital ways; that if noncoital methods of sex relations are employed, it is all right for the female to engage in fellation but that no real male would ever participate in cunnilinctus; that the girl should remain an absolute virgin until she is married while the boy should have as many sex adventures as possible; that it is a far greater crime for a female to have a child out of wedlock than it is for a male to father such a child; and that if a wife commits adultery it is a heinous offense against morality while if a husband is adulterous he is merely following his natural human bent (Masters and Lea, 1964).

All these beliefs of the sexual fascist, precisely like those of his politically fascist brother, are completely arbitrary and scientifically groundless. Women are not necessarily radically different from males in their sex desires; and, when they are, they are sometimes *more* rather than *less* highly sexed than men. It is, usually, important that they achieve regular orgasms; and it is more important, in many instances, that they achieve these orgasms by extracoital techniques than that the male enjoy noncoital sex play: because literally millions of women find it virtually impossible to come to climax during intercourse while they can fairly easily do so through clitoral manipulation, cunnilinctus, and other noncoital methods.

The notion that a girl should remain a virgin until marriage and is a far greater criminal than a male if she has a child out of wedlock or commits adultery is a most anti-equalitarian view that largely stems from the patriarchal customs of Biblical days and has no place in a democratic society. Women, of course, are the child-bearing sex; but they obviously cannot bear children without male collaboration, and should therefore assume no more and no less responsibility for premarital or extramarital "illegitimacy" than their paramours. To discriminate against females for their sex acts because they carry the biological burden of childbirth makes as much sense as punishing female thieves or murderers more severely than male criminals because the former, as potential or actual mothers, have greater responsibilities and presumably should therefore know better than to commit crimes.

The second major facet of sexual authoritarianism which we shall now discuss is another that stems almost directly from politico-economic fascist ideologies: namely, the demand for rigid conformity to a single, all-encompassing sex code for many different kinds of individuals.

Politico-social fascism, let it be remembered in this connection, almost always goes in for monolithic moral codes. The grand patriarch or monarch of a tribe or nation usually decides that what is right *for him* is right for *all;* and, willy-nilly, he crams his preferences down the throats of his adherents.

So, too, the sexual fascist. Either he is bigotedly raised to abide by a straight and narrow set of sex mores and laws and, doing so, he never practices any other mode; or he does, for a period of time, try various sex acts which do not conform to the code under which he was raised but, especially as older age and dimmed sexuality take their toll on his proclivities, he finally reverts to or newly invents some rigid rules of sex morality. In either event, he dogmatically decides that what is good enough for him is good enough for everyone—and they'd damned well better agree that it is or else.

This means that the sexual fascist arbitrarily defines other people's worth in direct proportion to the extent with which they conform to certain sex codes which he has unthinkingly adopted as "good" ones. If these other people conform closely to these codes, or agree with what *he* thinks they should do sexually, they are accepted as "good," "moral," "worthwhile" humans; and if they do not conform to the codes he deems to be correct, they are condemned as "wicked," "immoral," or "worthless." Here again, he is following the fascistic philosophy of measuring people's worth not in terms of their humanity, or what they are, but in terms of how well they do—or in this case do not do—certain things.

Forcing human beings to conform to almost any constricted pattern of living is an authoritarian and anti-democratic procedure because the very first law of human behavior is that of individual difference. Living things differ from inanimate objects in several basic ways: particularly that they have some freedom of action or movement, some ability to reproduce themselves, and some individuality or uniqueness. To the extent that their individuality is ignored, hampered, or restricted men and women become that less human.

In regard to their sexuality, men and women are notably different. Some have enormous sex drives, some little or no erotic impulses. Some enjoy the same kind of sex play or coitus almost all the time, others demand a large variety of sex acts and positions for their maximum satisfaction. Some find more and more enjoyment with the same partner, others find monogamous relations dull and boring.

The hallmark of emotional health for most human beings, moreover, is their maintaining a reasonable degree of flexibility and freedom from fixation in the major aspects of their lives. A few individuals may be truly happy if they rigidly stick to one limited job or a few basic foods all their lives; but the great majority of persons who are "content" to limit themselves in these ways are actually compulsively or fetishistically driven to do so by conscious or unconscious fears. These individuals are generally *afraid* to try to get out of their vocational or dietary ruts—irrationally afraid that they might fail in a new job or be nauseated by novel foods. Out of their irrational fears, they cravenly surrender a good deal of their potential life space, and fixatedly avail themselves of a minority of the pleasures and adventures of living that might theoretically be theirs.

So, again, with sex. The emotionally healthy individual is not one who fearfully and compulsively sticks to a very limited mode of satisfaction which he happened to hit upon fairly early in his sex development. Nor is he a person who convulsively or rebelliously has to keep trying every possible sex variation in or out of the books, largely because he cannot relaxedly enjoy sex participation for its own sake but must frantically and jadedly keep seeking for extrinsic "thrills." No: the unneurotic, undeviated sex participant is one who openmindedly and unfearingly tries a wide variety of practices, and finally ends up by adhering largely to relatively few of these acts which he has, by personal experience and observation, found to be maximally satisfying *to him*.

The philosophy and practice of the sex fascist, however, does not permit to any reasonable degree the sex adventurousness and experimentation which is normal to healthy, individually autonomous humans. It does its best—or worst—to force *all* persons into a single, invariant mold. In our own society, this one-sided brand of legally and socially allowable sex conduct has consisted of heterosexual coitus in one or two "natural" positions between a man and a woman who are formally married to each other. All other forms of sex behavior, such as masturbation, petting, premarital intercourse, or non-coital relations between husbands and wives, have been seriously frowned upon and encrusted with guilt; or else, as in the case of such acts as adultery and homosexuality, they have often been subject to fine and imprisonment.

Fascist ideologies have particularly prevailed in the sex areas while they have been relatively milder in many other aspects of social "misbehavior." Thus, we have considered an individual to be unmannerly or impolite if he does not follow certain rules of etiquette, such as eating or dressing in a decorous way. And we have looked upon a man or woman as vice-ridden if he or she is seriously addicted to, say, smoking, drinking, gluttony, or slothfulness. But in regard to most forms of so-called impoliteness and vice we have leveled only minor criticism or social sanction. In regard to sexual "vice," however, we have been savagely proscriptive and penalizing—just as political fascists, when they have power, generally are against the "vices" of individualism and non-conformity to their views.

The whole philosophy of excoriating and punishing human beings for their "sins" is, in fact, a fascist attitude which stems directly from primitive patriarchism. If a patriarch, monarch, or primitive deity lays down a set of rules of behavior, and someone in his jurisdiction flouts these rules, he never thinks in terms of the real problem—which, simply stated, is: How can I induce this rebellious individual to desist from breaking my rules *in the future*—but he is invariably so *personally* aggrieved that he only thinks in terms of: How can I punish that dirty so-and-so for his *past* and *present* impiety?

The fascist, in other words, is not really interested in

inducing people to avoid repeating their mistakes or to change their future behavior for the better. He is interested not in *them* but in *himself*—in his own (arbitrary) beliefs and how he can force people to conform to *his* dogmatisms. Similarly, the sex fascist is not in the least interested, really, in what modes of sex conduct would be best—meaning, least self-defeating and most satisfaction-producing—for people to follow. He is only autistically concerned with what codes *he insists they should* follow.

In consequence, the sex fascist can only think in terms of how different from *his* recommendations are the actions of those who masturbate, fornicate, pet to orgasm, etc. And instead of, at most, legislating against sex practices such as rape or the seduction of minors —which might well be harmful when perpetrated by one individual against another, he legislates or fumes against many sex modes which are matters of personal taste and preference, and which are not in the least antisocial as they are normally practiced.

A third significant aspect of sexual fascism is that which stems directly from and is linked inextricably with intellectual fascism. The intellectual fascist, as we previously noted, is an individual who insists that human beings are only worthwhile in relation to how well they perform, how competent, effective, and achieving they are. The sexual fascist applies this yardstick of intrinsic human worth to sex, love, and marital relationships.

More specifically, the sexual fascist views anyone—

including, ironically, himself—as a worthless, value-less individual unless he or she is perfectly sexually competent. This means, in the case of a male, that the "worthwhile'" individual has to be able to achieve an erection without any difficulty, to maintain it for a long period of time, and to be able, finally, to have an orgasm exactly at the same moment that his female partner has her climax. Preferably, moreover, the male should be able to become sexually aroused again shortly after he has had his initial orgasm, and to be capable of several climaxes a night. In addition, he should be able to arouse even the most recalcitrant female by his adept technique of sexual foreplay, and should be able to keep arousing her so that she has several orgasms in quick succession and thinks he is the greatest lover in the world.

The sexually adequate female, according to this intellectually fascistic view, is one who is able to be aroused to a high fever pitch of excitement in short order; who can easily have an orgasm after a brief period of intercourse; who can hold off her climax, if necessary, to match the moment when her male partner has his; and who is adept at every conceivable kind of sex play and enjoys all kinds of noncoital techniques, especially fellation. Such a woman, again, is able to have many terrific orgasms per evening and to be satisfied when her lover is finally surfeited.

This fascistic view of sexual adequacy is completely unrealistic in that, like some of the other authoritarian views we have been examining, it ignores the basic

172

facts of individual human differences. It fails to take note of the facts that many men and women are not great sex athletes; that sexual lasting powers differ enormously; that many sexually competent females do not have orgasms during coitus and many males are normally rapid firers in their sex actions; that some individuals who are excellent lovers are not unusual responders and that some who respond beautifully have little interest in making active love themselves.

More importantly, this perfectionistic view of sexual adequacy contains the basic fascistic assumption that if one is *not* uncommonly good at coital and non-coital sex play, one is essentially a nincompoop and a louse, and one might just as well curl up and die. It utterly ignores the truth that no man or woman can be competent or effective in all respects, nor even in all major respects, and that many worthwhile humans have little or no sex desire, technique, or capacity.

Let us consider a specific case, to see what the results of this kind of sexual fascism often are. Several years ago I saw for psychotherapy a young man whose main occupation in life appeared to be having affairs with females. He was unusually handsome and could speak well, so he had no difficulty in finding one partner after another.

Whenever he described his sex adventures to me, this individual invariably spoke in a highly deprecating tone about his girlfriend of the moment. This one looked fine when she was all dressed up; but she was "disgustingly titless" when she took off her clothes. That

173

one was "absolutely beautiful, from tip to stern"; but "she must have had a chunk of lead in her ass, and just lay there on the bed without even a wriggle, expecting me to do all the work." This new girl "stunk like a carload of pigs"; the one before that "was so inhibited that she couldn't be oral with a lollipop"; the one before her "was so bad in bed that a board with a hole in it would have been more exciting"; and so on and so forth.

Always, with rare exceptions, the sex partners of this young man would be described in highly negative terms as far as sex proclivities went; and the impression was given that since these girls were coitally or extra-coitally inept, they were perfectly worthless as human beings, and could very well drop dead for all he cared. No attention was given to the problem of possibly educating his partners, so that they might become better bedmates; and no inkling was given that they might have any non-sexual traits that might somewhat redeem their erotic deficiencies.

As it happened, this deprecator of young womanhood eventually met a girl who could give him cards and spades in nocturnal gymnastics and who would keep coming back for more. Whether lightly caressed or vigorously taken, she had no difficulty in getting one tremendous orgasm after another; and the active or passive sex participations which she did not thoroughly enjoy seemed to be almost nonexistent.

After seeing this paragon of feminine sexuality for a period of a few weeks, my patient began to notice a serious decrement in his own desires and powers. Fre-

quently, he found himself unable to maintain a sufficiently adequate erection to complete copulation; and
at other times, when he was sufficiently potent, he
found coitus to be joyless and non-climactic. Noting this
increasing degree of sexual incompetency on his part,
he began to become acutely depressed, and it was
only by forcing him to face and question the innermost
roots of his intellectual and sexual fascism that I was
able to help him overcome his neurotic condition.

For this individual, like the typical intellectual fascist, tended to define *all* human inadequacy and imper-
fection, including his own, as horrible and frightful.
Needing to appear superior to others, he felt continually
impelled to belittle the girls with whom he had affairs
—and whom, unconsciously, he often picked just because he could eventually focus on their deficiencies
and show them up. When he finally met his own sexual
match, he could no more tolerate his girl's compara-
tive competence than he could previously tolerate the
relative ineffectuality of his earlier girlfriends. For, according to his fascist-based personal ideology, he *had*
to be best, *had* to be supreme himself and no effective
competition to his grandiose claims could be borne.

The more my patient began to see that he was not
sexually peerless, he began to hate himself for his own
inadequacies; and the more he focused on and told
himself how horrible it was for him to be impotent or
inept, the more incompetent he became. This kind of
vicious neurotic circle can only be broken when the af-
flicted individual is able to see the fundamental irra-

175

tional assumptions or beliefs which underlie his disordered behavior. In this instance, when I finally was able to induce this young man to admit and to question his fascistic, perfectionistic ideas of sexual adequacy, and to stop measuring his and others' intrinsic value as human beings in terms of how notable was his or their sexual prowess, he stopped trying to keep up with his unusually high-sexed partner, and his potency returned. He also started to question his entire attitude toward females and their sexual propensities and to see them more as human beings than as mere bedmates.

To summarize what we have been discussing in this chapter: There are at least three major kinds of sexual fascism. The first type, which consists largely of discrimination by males against the sex rights and privileges of females, stems directly from primitive patriarchism and from contemporary politico-economic Nazi-fascism. The second type, consisting of the censoring and penalizing of harmless sex acts which run counter to some arbitrary authoritarian prejudice, also stems from political fascism, with undertones deriving from intellectual fascism. The third type, which views sexual inadequacy or incompetence as a heinous, unforgivable crime, derives from unrealistic, perfection-bent intellectual fascism.

All three of these main brands of sexual fascism have in common a demand that human beings, in their sex behavior, rigidly and invariantly conform to a certain kind of practice which is arbitrarily defined as "good" and that they refrain from other participations which are arbitrarily defined as "weak," wicked," or "bad." All three brands utterly refuse to admit that human beings are worthwhile, valuable individuals in their own right—just because they are human, because they exist.

Until we consistently acknowledge the intrinsic merit of ourselves and our fellows just because we *are* human, we *are* alive, politico-economic and intellectual fascism are bound to survive—and with them, their sexual fascistic derivatives. Until we accept people for *being* rather than being *something*, for *doing* rather than for doing *well*, all our vaunted liberalism and democracy will be babble. At bottom, we shall still be fascists.

15.

The Right to Sex Enjoyment

The time has come to recapitulate some of the main points that have been made in this book.

If I were, in a single sentence, to summarize the gist of what I have been saying, that sentence would read something like this: Every human being, just because he exists, should have the right to as much (or as little), as varied (or as monotonous), as intense (or as mild), as enduring (or as brief) sex enjoyments as he prefers —as long as, in the process of acquiring these preferred satisfactions, he does not needlessly, forcefully, or unfairly interfere with the sexual (or non-sexual) rights and satisfactions of others.

This means, more specifically, that in my estimation society should not legislate or invoke social sanctions against sex acts performed by individuals who are reasonably competent and well-educated adults; who use no force or duress in the course of their sex relations; who do not, without the consent of their partners, specifically injure these partners; and who participate in their sex activities privately, out of sight and sound of unwilling observers.

If this and only this kind of limitation were applied in modern communities, only a few distinct sex acts would be considered to be illegal or illegitimate. Included among these antisocial activities would be seduction of a minor by an adult; rape; sexual assault and murder; and exhibitionism or other forms of public display (Guyon, 1934, 1963).

Assuming that only these types of sex participations

178

should be legally banned, are there any other kinds which should be permissible and yet which individuals should personally abjure? There certainly are.

The sane and sound individual should normally refrain from engaging in any form of sex behavior which is self-defeating or self-injurious. More concretely: he or she should consider as undesirable or neurotic all sex participations which (a) cause personal physical injury (e.g., extreme sexual masochism); (b) are psychologically constricting or maiming (e.g., being the passive, dependent partner in a heterosexual or homosexual relationship); (c) are relatively unsatisfactory or uninteresting (e.g., exclusive resort to masturbation when heterosexual activities are available); (d) are largely motivated by anxiety, hostility, or other neurotic feelings rather than by honest preference (e.g., compulsive peeping used as a substitute for dating); or (e) are inimical to nonsexual desires and needs which one considers to be more important than sexual gratifications (e.g., having an adulterous affair at the real risk of ruining one's happy marital and family life).

In actual practice (alas!), our own society is such that, in order to live successfully within its laws and mores, the average highly sexed individual has to curb not merely many but probably the overwhelming majority of his sex desires and practices.

Even if such an individual chooses to remain unmarried all his life, and thus to avoid complicating sexual alliances, he must, if he is to remain out of jail, avoid all sex contacts with members of his own sex, with animals, and with underage members of the other sex; and,

179

in addition, he must not force his sexual attentions on others, engage in public sex acts, walk around indecorously clad, distribute so-called pornographic pictures or writings, etc., etc.

Quite aside from these legal restrictions, a normal member of our culture must curb his sex appetites and participations so that they do not too seriously offend the sensibilities of his relatives, friends, lovers, neighbors, and employers. If he does not exert at least a reasonable amount of control over his inclinations he will often find himself in socio-economic difficulties and in many instances will thereby do himself more harm than good.

If what has just been said is accurate, it should be apparent that the average, and particularly the highly sexed, individual in our culture is, sexually speaking, in a pretty kettle of paradoxes.

On the one hand, he theoretically has the right to engage in any preferential sex acts which are not injurious to others—which seems to leave him very wide latitude. But, on the other hand, if he is wise enough to abide by his human sex rights he may be foolish enough to perform several actions which, because of his society's antisexual attitudes, may lead to sorry consequences. What, under the circumstances, can the poor devil do?

The first thing he can do is to rid himself of the unnecessary or superfluous restrictions which society seems to be imposing on him but which, in the last analysis, he actually imposes on himself. Granted that it would be wrong for him literally to force himself on others or harm them sexually. Granted, also, that it

180

would be silly of him to engage in sex acts, such as intercourse with a fully developed but technically underage girl, whose true immorality may be debatable but for which he is likely to be legally penalized.

The fact remains, however, that there arc a good many other sex affairs which, although socially disapproved in our culture, *actually* carry no penalty but this very disapproval. And if an individual can inure himself—as virtually everyone can—against being affected by verbal and gestural condemnation of what he honestly considers to be his own perfectly harmless sex behavior, he can largely disarm others' carping and render their censure void (Clough, 1962; Ellis, 1962a, 1963e).

Take, for example, masturbation, petting, and premarital coitus. All these activities are highly disapproved by literally millions of individuals in our society. And other millions, in consequence, refrain from engaging in them, or else participate with considerable guilt.

If, however, a given person does not *want* to refrain from or to be guilty about autoerotism, petting to orgasm, or antenuptial affairs, there is no reason why he *need* refrain or be guilty. For these are the kind of activities which, today, *only* result in verbal or ideational disapprobation but which do not lead to specific other penalties.

Thus, even if your relatives, friends, and business associates know full well, in present-day America, that you masturbate, pet, or fornicate it is most unlikely that they will throw you out of the house, cut you dead in

181

the street, or fire you from your job. Occasionally, if they are sufficiently disturbed, they might invoke such real penalties; but this, at present, would be rare. Mostly, they would merely *think* and *talk* their disapproval.

You therefore have two good possibilities in dealing with people who disagree with one's harmless sex activities: (a) discreetly refrain from letting them know about these activities; or (b) let them know full well what your sex life is, but not give a fig when they disapprove.

Ordinarily social disapproval is, in other words, only hurtful in direct proportion to your *own* vulnerability to it. And if you would, after due consideration, have the courage to disagree with what others think of your sex behavior, and *not to take seriously* what they think, you would find it almost impossible to become upset by sexual condemnation—except, as we noted before, when this condemnation is forcefully backed by legal or socio-economic penalties: as, fortunately, it rarely is today.

The other effective action you can take to counteract unnecessary or superfluous restrictions on sexual behavior is to write, speak, draw, sing, choreograph and generally use whatever means of personal and mass communication you command to propagandize against the silly, humanity-sabotaging social disapproval that still exists in connection with many perfectly harmless, satisfying, voluntarily performed sex acts.

Already, as compared to previous centuries and decades, societal condemnation of innocuous sex pleasures has considerably decreased.

THE RIGHT TO SEX ENJOYMENT

If a sufficient number of Americans believe, as I do, that truly harmful and antisocial sex behavior should be curbed, but that other sex participations should be, if anything, encouraged; and if enough of these sexual democrats openly say, by their words and deeds, what they believe, our antiquated, anti-human antisexual codes will more quickly and profoundly wither away (Hefner, 1962-65; Young, 1964).

To conclude: Every human being should certainly refrain from sex participations which needlessly, forcefully, or unfairly harm others. And each of us, if we are to remain rational and non-neurotic, should cease and desist from all sex behavior which is clearly self-defeating.

Over and above this, everyone has a human right to sex-love involvement of his own taste, preference, and inclination. And the more he speaks and fights for that right, the more, in practice, he (or she!) is likely to realize and enjoy it.

BIBLIOGRAPHY

Arlington, Norman. "Sexual starvation in the American male." *Independent*. Oct. 1958, Issue 81, 1, 8.

Beigel, Hugo. "Illegitimacy." See Ellis and Abarbanel, 1961.

Beigel, Hugo. *Sex from A to Z*. New York: Ungar, 1962.

Benjamin, Harry, and Masters, R. E. L. *Prostitution and morality*. New York: Julian, 1964.

Bergler, Edmund. *Counterfeit-sex*. New York: Grove Press, 1961.

Bieber, Irving, et al. *Homosexuality*. New York: Basic Books, 1962.

Bohm, Ewald, and Johnstadt, Trygve. "Sex life of Scandinavian countries." See Ellis and Abarbanel, 1961.

Brown, Helen Gurley. *Sex and the single girl*. New York: Geis, 1962.

Brown, Helen Gurley. *Sex in the office*. New York: Geis, 1964.

Caprio, Frank S. *The sexually adequate male*. New York: Citadel, 1960.

Chesser, Eustace. *The sexual, marital and family relationships of the English woman*. New York: Roy, 1956.

Clark, LeMon. "A doctor looks at self relief." *Sexology*, 1958, 24, 785-788.

Clough, Eric. *The outraged*. Burlingame, Calif.: Author, 1962.

Comfort, Alex. *Sexual behavior in society*. London: Duckworth, 1950.

Cory, Donald Webster. *The homosexual in America*. New York: Paperback Library, 1963.

Cory, Donald Webster, and Leroy, J. P. *The homosexual and his society*. New York: Citadel, 1963.

Davis, Katherine B. *Factors in the sex life of 2200 women*. New York: Harper, 1929.

Dearborn, Lester W. "Autoerotism." See Ellis and Abarbanel, 1961.

deRachewiltz, Boris. *Black eros*. New York: Lyle Stuart, 1964.

Dickinson, Robert L., and Beam, L. *A thousand marriages*. Baltimore: Williams and Wilkins, 1931.

Duvall, Evelyn M. *Love and the facts of life*. New York: Association Press, 1963.

Edwardes, Allen, and Masters, R. E. L. *The cradle of erotica*. New York: Julian, 1962.

Ehrmann, Winston W. *Premarital dating behavior*. New York: Holt, 1960.

Ellis, Albert. "What is normal sex behavior?" *Complex*, 1952, 8, 41-51. Reprinted in Ellis and Brancale.

Ellis, Albert. "Female sexual response and marital relations." *Soc. Problems*, 1954, 1, 152-155.

Ellis, Albert. *How to live with a neurotic*. New York: Crown, 1957.

Ellis, Albert. *The art and science of love*. New York: Lyle Stuart, 1960.

Ellis, Albert. "Coitus." See Ellis and Abarbanel, 1961.

Ellis, Albert. *Reason and emotion in psychotherapy*. New York: Lyle Stuart, 1962a.

Ellis, Albert. *The folklore of sex*. New York: Grove Press, 1962b.

Ellis, Albert. *Sex and the single man*. New York: Lyle Stuart, 1963a.

Ellis, Albert. *The intelligent woman's guide to manhunting*. New York: Lyle Stuart, 1963b.

Ellis, Albert. *The American sexual tragedy*. New York: Lyle Stuart, 1962. New York: Grove Press, 1963c.

Ellis, Albert. *If this be sexual heresy . . .* New York: Lyle Stuart, 1963d.

Ellis, Albert. *The origins and the development of the incest taboo*. New York: Lyle Stuart, 1963e.

Ellis, Albert. *The case for sexual liberty*. Vol. I. Tucson: Seymour Press, 1965a.

Ellis, Albert. *Homosexuality: its causes and cure*. New York: Lyle Stuart, 1965b.

Ellis, Albert. *Suppressed: seven key essays publishers dared not print*. Chicago: New Classics House, 1965c.

Ellis, Albert, and Abarbanel, Albert. *The encyclopedia of sexual behavior*. Two volumes. New York: Hawthorn Books, 1961.

Ellis, Albert, and Brancale, Ralph. *The psychology of sex offenders*. Springfield, Illinois: Charles C Thomas, 1956

Ellis, Albert, and Harper, Robert A. *A guide to rational living*. Englewood Cliffs, N.J.: Prentice-Hall, 1961a.

Ellis, Albert, and Harper, Robert A. *Creative marriage*. New York: Lyle Stuart, 1961b.

Ellis, Albert, and Sagarin, Edward *Nymphomania: a study of the oversexed woman*. New York: Gilbert Press-Julian Messner, Inc., 1964.

Ellis, Havelock. *Studies in the psychology of sex.* Two volumes. New York: Random House, 1936.

Epton, Nina. *Love and the English.* New York: Collier, 1962.

Ford, Clellan S., and Beach, Frank A. *Patterns of sexual behavior.* New York: Ace, 1962.

Freud, Sigmund. *Collected papers.* Five volumes. London: Imago, 1924-1950.

Freud, Sigmund. *Basic writings.* New York: Modern Library, 1938.

Fromm, Erich. *The art of loving.* New York: Bantam Books, 1963.

Gichner, Lawrence. *Erotic aspects of Hindu culture.* Washington, D.C.: Author, 1957.

Gichner, Lawrence. *Erotic aspects of Japanese culture.* Washington, D.C.: Author, 1958.

Grant, Vernon. *Psychology of sexual emotion.* New York: Longmans, 1957.

Guyon, Rene. *The ethics of sexual acts.* New York: Knopf, 1934.

Guyon, Rene. "The case against chastity and virginity." See Ellis and Abarbanel, 1961.

Guyon, Rene. *A case for sexual freedom.* Hollywood: France International Publications, 1963.

Hamilton, G. V. *A research in marriage.* New York: Boni, 1929.

Harper, Robert A. "Petting." See Ellis and Abarbanel, 1961a.

Harper, Robert A. "Extramarital sex relations." See Ellis and Abarbanel, 1961b.

Hefner, Hugh. "The playboy philosophy." *Playboy,* 1962-1965.

Hegeler, Inge, and Hegeler, Sten. *An ABZ of love.* London: Spearman, 1963.

Hirsch, Edwin W. *The power to love.* New York: Pyramid, 1961.

Hirsch, Edwin W. *Sexual fear.* New York: Pyramid, 1962.

Hunt, Morton M. *The natural history of love.* New York: Grove Press, 1962.

Kegel, A. H. "Sexual functions of the pubococcygeus muscle." *West. J. Surg. Obst.,* 1952, 60, 521-524.

Kegel, A. H. "Early genital relaxation." *Obstet. & Gynecol.,* 1956, 8, No. 5.

Kelly, G. Lombard. *Sex manual for those married or about to be.* Augusta, Ga.: Southern Medical Supply Co., 1953.

Kelly, G. Lombard. *So you think you're impotent!* Augusta, Ga.: Southern Medical Supply Co., 1957.

Kinsey, Alfred C., et al. *Sexual behavior in the human male.* Philadelphia: Saunders, 1948.

Kinsey, Alfred C., et al. *Sexual behavior in the human female.* Philadelphia: Saunders, 1953.

Kirkendall, Lester A. *Premarital intercourse and inter-personal relationships.* New York: Julian, 1961.

Kronhausen, Eberhard, and Kronhausen, Phyllis. *Sex histories of American college men.* New York: Ballantine, 1960.

Kronhausen, Phyllis, and Kronhausen, Eberhard. *The sexually responsive woman.* New York: Grove Press, 1964.

Leader, A. Quoted in Secor, H. W. "Sex frustration." *Sexology,* 1959, 25, 480-483.

Mace, David R. "The case for chastity and virginity." See Ellis and Abarbanel, 1961.

Malla, Kalayana. *Ananga ranga: the Hindu art of love.* New York: Medical Press, 1964.

Masters, R. E. L., and Lea, Eduard. *The anti-sex.* New York: Julian, 1964.

Masters, William H., and Johnson, Virginia E. "The anatomy of female orgasm." See Ellis and Abarbanel, 1961.

Masters, William H., and Johnson, Virginia E. "The sexual response cycle of the human female. III. The clitoris: anatomic and clinical considerations." *West. J. Surg. Obstet. & Gynecol.,* 1962, 270, 248-257.

Mead, Margaret. *From the south seas.* New York: Morrow, 1939.

Nefzawi, Mohammed al. *Perfumed garden.* New York: Medical Press, 1964.

Reevy, William. "Adolescent sexuality." See Ellis and Abarbanel, 1961.

Reich, Wilhelm. *Function of the orgasm.* New York: Noonday Press, 1961.

Reich, Wilhelm. *The sexual revolution.* New York: Noonday Press, 1962.

Reiss, Ira L. *Premarital sexual standards in America.* Glencoe: Free Press, 1960.

Riesman, David, et al. *The lonely crowd.* New Haven: Yale University Press, 1961.

Robinson, Marie N. *The power of sexual surrender.* New York: New American Library, 1962.

Sorokin, Pitirim. *The American sex revolution*. Boston: Sargent, 1956.

Spitz, Rene A. "Autoerotism." *Psychoanalytic Study of the Child*. 1949, 3-4, 85-120.

Stearn, Jess. *The sixth man*. New York: Macfadden, 1963.

Stekel, Wilhelm. *Autoerotism*. New York: Liveright, 1950.

Stokes, Walter R. "Our changing sex ethics." *Marr. Fam. Living*. 1962, 24, 269-272.

Tatum, Brooking. "Can nudism afford its wife swappers?" *Eden*, No. 16, 1964, 17-21.

Taylor, G. Rattray. *Sex in history*. New York: Ballantine, 1962.

Taylor, William S. "A critique of sublimation in males." *Genet. Psychology Monographs*, 1933, 13, 1-115.

Terman, Lewis M. *Psychological factors in marital unhappiness*. New York: McGraw-Hill, 1938.

Terman, Lewis M. "Correlates of orgasm adequacy in a group of 556 wives." *J. Psychol.*, 1951, 32, 115-172.

Van Emde Boas, Conrad. "Sex life in Europe." See Ellis and Abarbanel, 1961.

Waldemar, Charles. *The mystery of sex*. New York: Lyle Stuart, 1960.

Young, Wayland. *Eros denied*. New York: Grove Press, 1964.

MELVIN POWERS SELF-IMPROVEMENT LIBRARY

ASTROLOGY
____ ASTROLOGY: HOW TO CHART YOUR HOROSCOPE *Max Heindel*	5.00
____ ASTROLOGY AND SEXUAL ANALYSIS *Morris C. Goodman*	5.00
____ ASTROLOGY AND YOU *Carroll Righter*	5.00
____ ASTROLOGY MADE EASY *Astarte*	7.00
____ ASTROLOGY, ROMANCE, YOU AND THE STARS *Anthony Norvell*	5.00
____ MY WORLD OF ASTROLOGY *Sydney Omarr*	7.00
____ THOUGHT DIAL *Sydney Omarr*	7.00
____ WHAT THE STARS REVEAL ABOUT THE MEN IN YOUR LIFE *Thelma White*	3.00

BRIDGE
____ BRIDGE BIDDING MADE EASY *Edwin B. Kantar*	10.00
____ BRIDGE CONVENTIONS *Edwin B. Kantar*	10.00
____ COMPETITIVE BIDDING IN MODERN BRIDGE *Edgar Kaplan*	7.00
____ DEFENSIVE BRIDGE PLAY COMPLETE *Edwin B. Kantar*	20.00
____ GAMESMAN BRIDGE—PLAY BETTER WITH KANTAR *Edwin B. Kantar*	7.00
____ HOW TO IMPROVE YOUR BRIDGE *Alfred Sheinwold*	7.00
____ IMPROVING YOUR BIDDING SKILLS *Edwin B. Kantar*	7.00
____ INTRODUCTION TO DECLARER'S PLAY *Edwin B. Kantar*	7.00
____ INTRODUCTION TO DEFENDER'S PLAY *Edwin B. Kantar*	7.00
____ KANTAR FOR THE DEFENSE *Edwin B. Kantar*	7.00
____ KANTAR FOR THE DEFENSE VOLUME 2 *Edwin B. Kantar*	7.00
____ TEST YOUR BRIDGE PLAY *Edwin B. Kantar*	7.00
____ VOLUME 2—TEST YOUR BRIDGE PLAY *Edwin B. Kantar*	7.00
____ WINNING DECLARER PLAY *Dorothy Hayden Truscott*	10.00

BUSINESS, STUDY & REFERENCE
____ BRAINSTORMING *Charles Clark*	10.00
____ CONVERSATION MADE EASY *Elliot Russell*	5.00
____ EXAM SECRET *Dennis B. Jackson*	5.00
____ FIX-IT BOOK *Arthur Symons*	2.00
____ HOW TO DEVELOP A BETTER SPEAKING VOICE *M. Hellier*	5.00
____ HOW TO SAVE 50% ON GAS & CAR EXPENSES *Ken Stansbie*	5.00
____ HOW TO SELF-PUBLISH YOUR BOOK & MAKE IT A BEST SELLER *Melvin Powers*	20.00
____ INCREASE YOUR LEARNING POWER *Geoffrey A. Dudley*	5.00
____ PRACTICAL GUIDE TO BETTER CONCENTRATION *Melvin Powers*	5.00
____ 7 DAYS TO FASTER READING *William S. Schaill*	7.00
____ SONGWRITERS' RHYMING DICTIONARY *Jane Shaw Whitfield*	10.00
____ SPELLING MADE EASY *Lester D. Basch & Dr. Milton Finkelstein*	3.00
____ STUDENT'S GUIDE TO BETTER GRADES *J. A. Rickard*	3.00
____ TEST YOURSELF—FIND YOUR HIDDEN TALENT *Jack Shafer*	3.00
____ YOUR WILL & WHAT TO DO ABOUT IT *Attorney Samuel G. Kling*	5.00

CALLIGRAPHY
____ ADVANCED CALLIGRAPHY *Katherine Jeffares*	7.00
____ CALLIGRAPHY—THE ART OF BEAUTIFUL WRITING *Katherine Jeffares*	7.00
____ CALLIGRAPHY FOR FUN & PROFIT *Anne Leptich & Jacque Evans*	7.00
____ CALLIGRAPHY MADE EASY *Tina Serafini*	7.00

CHESS & CHECKERS
____ BEGINNER'S GUIDE TO WINNING CHESS *Fred Reinfeld*	7.00
____ CHESS IN TEN EASY LESSONS *Larry Evans*	10.00
____ CHESS MADE EASY *Milton L. Hanauer*	5.00
____ CHESS PROBLEMS FOR BEGINNERS *Edited by Fred Reinfeld*	5.00
____ CHESS TACTICS FOR BEGINNERS *Edited by Fred Reinfeld*	7.00

_____ HOW TO WIN AT CHECKERS *Fred Reinfeld*   5.00
_____ 1001 BRILLIANT WAYS TO CHECKMATE *Fred Reinfeld*   10.00
_____ 1001 WINNING CHESS SACRIFICES & COMBINATIONS *Fred Reinfeld*   10.00

COOKERY & HERBS

_____ CULPEPER'S HERBAL REMEDIES *Dr. Nicholas Culpeper*   5.00
_____ FAST GOURMET COOKBOOK *Poppy Cannon*   2.50
_____ HEALING POWER OF HERBS *May Bethel*   5.00
_____ HEALING POWER OF NATURAL FOODS *May Bethel*   7.00
_____ HERBS FOR HEALTH—HOW TO GROW & USE THEM *Louise Evans Doole*   5.00
_____ HOME GARDEN COOKBOOK—DELICIOUS NATURAL FOOD RECIPES *Ken Kraft*   3.00
_____ MEATLESS MEAL GUIDE *Tomi Ryan & James H. Ryan, M.D.*   4.00
_____ VEGETABLE GARDENING FOR BEGINNERS *Hugh Wiberg*   2.00
_____ VEGETABLES FOR TODAY'S GARDENS *R. Milton Carleton*   2.00
_____ VEGETARIAN COOKERY *Janet Walker*   7.00
_____ VEGETARIAN COOKING MADE EASY & DELECTABLE *Veronica Vezza*   3.00
_____ VEGETARIAN DELIGHTS—A HAPPY COOKBOOK FOR HEALTH *K. R. Mehta*   2.00

GAMBLING & POKER

_____ HOW TO WIN AT DICE GAMES *Skip Frey*   3.00
_____ HOW TO WIN AT POKER *Terence Reese & Anthony T. Watkins*   7.00
_____ SCARNE ON DICE *John Scarne*   15.00
_____ WINNING AT CRAPS *Dr. Lloyd T. Commins*   5.00
_____ WINNING AT GIN *Chester Wander & Cy Rice*   3.00
_____ WINNING AT POKER—AN EXPERT'S GUIDE *John Archer*   10.00
_____ WINNING AT 21—AN EXPERT'S GUIDE *John Archer*   7.00
_____ WINNING POKER SYSTEMS *Norman Zadeh*   3.00

HEALTH

_____ BEE POLLEN *Lynda Lyngheim & Jack Scagnetti*   5.00
_____ COPING WITH ALZHEIMER'S *Rose Oliver, Ph.D. & Francis Bock, Ph.D.*   10.00
_____ DR. LINDNER'S POINT SYSTEM FOOD PROGRAM *Peter G. Lindner, M.D.*   2.00
_____ HELP YOURSELF TO BETTER SIGHT *Margaret Darst Corbett*   7.00
_____ HOW YOU CAN STOP SMOKING PERMANENTLY *Ernest Caldwell*   5.00
_____ MIND OVER PLATTER *Peter G. Lindner, M.D.*   5.00
_____ NATURE'S WAY TO NUTRITION & VIBRANT HEALTH *Robert J. Scrutton*   3.00
_____ NEW CARBOHYDRATE DIET COUNTER *Patti Lopez-Pereira*   2.00
_____ REFLEXOLOGY *Dr. Maybelle Segal*   5.00
_____ REFLEXOLOGY FOR GOOD HEALTH *Anna Kaye & Don C. Matchan*   7.00
_____ 30 DAYS TO BEAUTIFUL LEGS *Dr. Marc Selner*   3.00
_____ WONDER WITHIN *Thomas F. Coyle, M.D.*   10.00
_____ YOU CAN LEARN TO RELAX *Dr. Samuel Gutwirth*   5.00

HOBBIES

_____ BEACHCOMBING FOR BEGINNERS *Norman Hickin*   2.00
_____ BLACKSTONE'S MODERN CARD TRICKS *Harry Blackstone*   7.00
_____ BLACKSTONE'S SECRETS OF MAGIC *Harry Blackstone*   5.00
_____ COIN COLLECTING FOR BEGINNERS *Burton Hobson & Fred Reinfeld*   7.00
_____ ENTERTAINING WITH ESP *Tony 'Doc' Shiels*   2.00
_____ 400 FASCINATING MAGIC TRICKS YOU CAN DO *Howard Thurston*   7.00
_____ HOW I TURN JUNK INTO FUN AND PROFIT *Sari*   3.00
_____ HOW TO WRITE A HIT SONG & SELL IT *Tommy Boyce*   10.00
_____ MAGIC FOR ALL AGES *Walter Gibson*   7.00
_____ STAMP COLLECTING FOR BEGINNERS *Burton Hobson*   3.00

HORSE PLAYER'S WINNING GUIDES

_____ BETTING HORSES TO WIN *Les Conklin*   7.00
_____ ELIMINATE THE LOSERS *Bob McKnight*   5.00
_____ HOW TO PICK WINNING HORSES *Bob McKnight*   5.00

___ HOW TO WIN AT THE RACES *Sam (The Genius) Lewin*	5.00
___ HOW YOU CAN BEAT THE RACES *Jack Kavanaqh*	5.00
___ MAKING MONEY AT THE RACES *David Barr*	5.00
___ PAYDAY AT THE RACES *Les Conklin*	5.00
___ SMART HANDICAPPING MADE EASY *William Bauman*	5.00
___ SUCCESS AT THE HARNESS RACES *Barry Meadow*	7.00

HUMOR

___ HOW TO FLATTEN YOUR TUSH *Coach Marge Reardon*	2.00
___ JOKE TELLER'S HANDBOOK *Bob Orben*	7.00
___ JOKES FOR ALL OCCASIONS *Al Schock*	5.00
___ 2,000 NEW LAUGHS FOR SPEAKERS *Bob Orben*	7.00
___ 2,400 JOKES TO BRIGHTEN YOUR SPEECHES *Robert Orben*	7.00
___ 2,500 JOKES TO START 'EM LAUGHING *Bob Orben*	10.00

HYPNOTISM

___ ADVANCED TECHNIQUES OF HYPNOSIS *Melvin Powers*	3.00
___ CHILDBIRTH WITH HYPNOSIS *William S. Kroger, M.D.*	5.00
___ HOW TO SOLVE YOUR SEX PROBLEMS WITH SELF-HYPNOSIS *Frank S. Caprio, M.D.*	5.00
___ HOW TO STOP SMOKING THRU SELF-HYPNOSIS *Leslie M. LeCron*	3.00
___ HOW YOU CAN BOWL BETTER USING SELF-HYPNOSIS *Jack Heise*	7.00
___ HOW YOU CAN PLAY BETTER GOLF USING SELF-HYPNOSIS *Jack Heise*	3.00
___ HYPNOSIS AND SELF-HYPNOSIS *Bernard Hollander, M.D.*	5.00
___ HYPNOTISM *(Originally published in 1893) Carl Sextus*	5.00
___ HYPNOTISM MADE EASY *Dr. Ralph Winn*	7.00
___ HYPNOTISM MADE PRACTICAL *Louis Orton*	5.00
___ HYPNOTISM REVEALED *Melvin Powers*	3.00
___ HYPNOTISM TODAY *Leslie LeCron and Jean Bordeaux, Ph.D.*	5.00
___ MODERN HYPNOSIS *Lesley Kuhn & Salvatore Russo, Ph.D.*	5.00
___ NEW CONCEPTS OF HYPNOSIS *Bernard C. Gindes, M.D.*	10.00
___ NEW SELF-HYPNOSIS *Paul Adams*	10.00
___ POST-HYPNOTIC INSTRUCTIONS—SUGGESTIONS FOR THERAPY *Arnold Furst*	10.00
___ PRACTICAL GUIDE TO SELF-HYPNOSIS *Melvin Powers*	5.00
___ PRACTICAL HYPNOTISM *Philip Magonet, M.D.*	3.00
___ SECRETS OF HYPNOTISM *S. J. Van Pelt, M.D.*	5.00
___ SELF-HYPNOSIS—A CONDITIONED-RESPONSE TECHNIQUE *Laurence Sparks*	7.00
___ SELF-HYPNOSIS—ITS THEORY, TECHNIQUE & APPLICATION *Melvin Powers*	3.00
___ THERAPY THROUGH HYPNOSIS *Edited by Raphael H. Rhodes*	5.00

JUDAICA

___ SERVICE OF THE HEART *Evelyn Garfiel, Ph.D.*	10.00
___ STORY OF ISRAEL IN COINS *Jean & Maurice Gould*	2.00
___ STORY OF ISRAEL IN STAMPS *Maxim & Gabriel Shamir*	1.00
___ TONGUE OF THE PROPHETS *Robert St. John*	10.00

JUST FOR WOMEN

___ COSMOPOLITAN'S GUIDE TO MARVELOUS MEN Foreword by *Helen Gurley Brown*	3.00
___ COSMOPOLITAN'S HANG-UP HANDBOOK Foreword by *Helen Gurley Brown*	4.00
___ COSMOPOLITAN'S LOVE BOOK—A GUIDE TO ECSTASY IN BED	7.00
___ COSMOPOLITAN'S NEW ETIQUETTE GUIDE Foreword by *Helen Gurley Brown*	4.00
___ I AM A COMPLEAT WOMAN *Doris Hagopian & Karen O'Connor Sweeney*	3.00
___ JUST FOR WOMEN—A GUIDE TO THE FEMALE BODY *Richard E. Sand, M.D.*	5.00
___ NEW APPROACHES TO SEX IN MARRIAGE *John E. Eichenlaub, M.D.*	3.00
___ SEXUALLY ADEQUATE FEMALE *Frank S. Caprio, M.D.*	3.00
___ SEXUALLY FULFILLED WOMAN *Dr. Rachel Copelan*	5.00

MARRIAGE, SEX & PARENTHOOD

____ ABILITY TO LOVE *Dr. Allan Fromme*	7.00
____ GUIDE TO SUCCESSFUL MARRIAGE *Drs. Albert Ellis & Robert Harper*	7.00
____ HOW TO RAISE AN EMOTIONALLY HEALTHY, HAPPY CHILD *Albert Ellis, Ph.D.*	10.00
____ PARENT SURVIVAL TRAINING *Marvin Silverman, Ed.D. & David Lustig, Ph.D.*	10.00
____ SEX WITHOUT GUILT *Albert Ellis, Ph.D.*	7.00
____ SEXUALLY ADEQUATE MALE *Frank S. Caprio, M.D.*	3.00
____ SEXUALLY FULFILLED MAN *Dr. Rachel Copelan*	5.00
____ STAYING IN LOVE *Dr. Norton F. Kristy*	7.00

MELVIN POWERS' MAIL ORDER LIBRARY

____ HOW TO GET RICH IN MAIL ORDER *Melvin Powers*	20.00
____ HOW TO SELF-PUBLISH YOUR BOOK & MAKE IT A BEST SELLER *Melvin Powers*	20.00
____ HOW TO WRITE A GOOD ADVERTISEMENT *Victor O. Schwab*	20.00
____ MAIL ORDER MADE EASY *J. Frank Brumbaugh*	20.00

METAPHYSICS & OCCULT

____ CONCENTRATION—A GUIDE TO MENTAL MASTERY *Mouni Sadhu*	7.00
____ EXTRA-TERRESTRIAL INTELLIGENCE—THE FIRST ENCOUNTER	6.00
____ FORTUNE TELLING WITH CARDS *P. Foli*	5.00
____ HOW TO INTERPRET DREAMS, OMENS & FORTUNE TELLING SIGNS *Gettings*	5.00
____ HOW TO UNDERSTAND YOUR DREAMS *Geoffrey A. Dudley*	5.00
____ IN DAYS OF GREAT PEACE *Mouni Sadhu*	3.00
____ MAGICIAN—HIS TRAINING AND WORK *W. E. Butler*	7.00
____ MEDITATION *Mouni Sadhu*	10.00
____ MODERN NUMEROLOGY *Morris C. Goodman*	5.00
____ NUMEROLOGY—ITS FACTS AND SECRETS *Ariel Yvon Taylor*	6.00
____ NUMEROLOGY MADE EASY *W. Mykian*	5.00
____ PALMISTRY MADE EASY *Fred Gettings*	5.00
____ PALMISTRY MADE PRACTICAL *Elizabeth Daniels Squire*	7.00
____ PROPHECY IN OUR TIME *Martin Ebon*	2.50
____ SUPERSTITION—ARE YOU SUPERSTITIOUS? *Eric Maple*	2.00
____ TAROT *Mouni Sadhu*	10.00
____ TAROT OF THE BOHEMIANS *Papus*	7.00
____ WAYS TO SELF-REALIZATION *Mouni Sadhu*	7.00
____ WITCHCRAFT, MAGIC & OCCULTISM—A FASCINATING HISTORY *W. B. Crow*	10.00
____ WITCHCRAFT—THE SIXTH SENSE *Justine Glass*	7.00

RECOVERY

____ KNIGHT IN RUSTY ARMOR *Robert Fisher*	5.00
____ KNIGHT IN RUSTY ARMOR *Robert Fisher (Hard cover edition)*	10.00

SELF-HELP & INSPIRATIONAL

____ CHARISMA—HOW TO GET "THAT SPECIAL MAGIC" *Marcia Grad*	7.00
____ DAILY POWER FOR JOYFUL LIVING *Dr. Donald Curtis*	7.00
____ DYNAMIC THINKING *Melvin Powers*	5.00
____ GREATEST POWER IN THE UNIVERSE *U. S. Andersen*	7.00
____ GROW RICH WHILE YOU SLEEP *Ben Sweetland*	8.00
____ GROW RICH WITH YOUR MILLION DOLLAR MIND *Brian Adams*	7.00
____ GROWTH THROUGH REASON *Albert Ellis, Ph.D.*	10.00
____ GUIDE TO PERSONAL HAPPINESS *Albert Ellis, Ph.D. & Irving Becker, Ed.D.*	10.00
____ HANDWRITING ANALYSIS MADE EASY *John Marley*	7.00
____ HANDWRITING TELLS *Nadya Olyanova*	7.00
____ HOW TO ATTRACT GOOD LUCK *A.H.Z. Carr*	7.00
____ HOW TO DEVELOP A WINNING PERSONALITY *Martin Panzer*	7.00
____ HOW TO DEVELOP AN EXCEPTIONAL MEMORY *Young & Gibson*	7.00
____ HOW TO LIVE WITH A NEUROTIC *Albert Ellis, Ph.D.*	7.00
____ HOW TO OVERCOME YOUR FEARS *M. P. Leahy, M.D.*	3.00
____ HOW TO SUCCEED *Brian Adams*	7.00

___ HUMAN PROBLEMS & HOW TO SOLVE THEM *Dr. Donald Curtis*		5.00
___ I CAN *Ben Sweetland*		8.00
___ I WILL *Ben Sweetland*		8.00
___ KNIGHT IN RUSTY ARMOR *Robert Fisher*		5.00
___ KNIGHT IN RUSTY ARMOR *Robert Fisher (Hard cover edition)*		10.00
___ LEFT-HANDED PEOPLE *Michael Barsley*		5.00
___ MAGIC IN YOUR MIND *U.S. Andersen*		10.00
___ MAGIC OF THINKING SUCCESS *Dr. David J. Schwartz*		8.00
___ MAGIC POWER OF YOUR MIND *Walter M. Germain*		7.00
___ MENTAL POWER THROUGH SLEEP SUGGESTION *Melvin Powers*		3.00
___ NEVER UNDERESTIMATE THE SELLING POWER OF A WOMAN *Dottie Walters*		7.00
___ NEW GUIDE TO RATIONAL LIVING *Albert Ellis, Ph.D. & R. Harper, Ph.D.*		10.00
___ PSYCHO-CYBERNETICS *Maxwell Maltz, M.D.*		7.00
___ PSYCHOLOGY OF HANDWRITING *Nadya Olyanova*		7.00
___ SALES CYBERNETICS *Brian Adams*		10.00
___ SCIENCE OF MIND IN DAILY LIVING *Dr. Donald Curtis*		7.00
___ SECRET OF SECRETS *U.S. Andersen*		7.00
___ SECRET POWER OF THE PYRAMIDS *U. S. Andersen*		7.00
___ SELF-THERAPY FOR THE STUTTERER *Malcolm Frazer*		3.00
___ SUCCESS-CYBERNETICS *U. S. Andersen*		7.00
___ 10 DAYS TO A GREAT NEW LIFE *William E. Edwards*		3.00
___ THINK AND GROW RICH *Napoleon Hill*		8.00
___ THINK LIKE A WINNER *Dr. Walter Doyle Staples*		10.00
___ THREE MAGIC WORDS *U. S. Andersen*		10.00
___ TREASURY OF COMFORT *Edited by Rabbi Sidney Greenberg*		10.00
___ TREASURY OF THE ART OF LIVING *Sidney S. Greenberg*		7.00
___ WHAT YOUR HANDWRITING REVEALS *Albert E. Hughes*		4.00
___ WONDER WITHIN *Thomas F. Coyle, M.D.*		10.00
___ YOUR SUBCONSCIOUS POWER *Charles M. Simmons*		7.00
___ YOUR THOUGHTS CAN CHANGE YOUR LIFE *Dr. Donald Curtis*		7.00

SPORTS

___ BILLIARDS—POCKET • CAROM • THREE CUSHION *Clive Cottingham, Jr.*		7.00
___ COMPLETE GUIDE TO FISHING *Vlad Evanoff*		2.00
___ HOW TO IMPROVE YOUR RACQUETBALL *Lubarsky, Kaufman & Scagnetti*		5.00
___ HOW TO WIN AT POCKET BILLIARDS *Edward D. Knuchell*		10.00
___ JOY OF WALKING *Jack Scagnetti*		3.00
___ LEARNING & TEACHING SOCCER SKILLS *Eric Worthington*		3.00
___ RACQUETBALL FOR WOMEN *Toni Hudson, Jack Scagnetti & Vince Rondone*		3.00
___ SECRET OF BOWLING STRIKES *Dawson Taylor*		5.00
___ SOCCER—THE GAME & HOW TO PLAY IT *Gary Rosenthal*		7.00
___ STARTING SOCCER *Edward F. Dolan, Jr.*		3.00

TENNIS LOVER'S LIBRARY

___ HOW TO BEAT BETTER TENNIS PLAYERS *Loring Fiske*		4.00
___ PSYCH YOURSELF TO BETTER TENNIS *Dr. Walter A. Luszki*		2.00
___ TENNIS FOR BEGINNERS *Dr. H. A. Murray*		2.00
___ TENNIS MADE EASY *Joel Brecheen*		5.00
___ WEEKEND TENNIS—HOW TO HAVE FUN & WIN AT THE SAME TIME *Bill Talbert*		3.00

WILSHIRE PET LIBRARY

___ DOG TRAINING MADE EASY & FUN *John W. Kellogg*		5.00
___ HOW TO BRING UP YOUR PET DOG *Kurt Unkelbach*		2.00
___ HOW TO RAISE & TRAIN YOUR PUPPY *Jeff Griffen*		5.00

The books listed above can be obtained from your book dealer or directly from Melvin Powers. When ordering, please remit $2.00 postage for the first book and $1.00 for each additional book.

Melvin Powers
12015 Sherman Road, No. Hollywood, California 91605

WILSHIRE HORSE LOVERS' LIBRARY

The books listed above can be obtained from your book dealer or directly from Melvin Powers. When ordering, please remit $2.00 postage for the first book and $1.00 for each additional book.

Melvin Powers
12015 Sherman Road, No. Hollywood, California 91605

HOW TO GET RICH IN MAIL ORDER
by Melvin Powers

1. How to Develop Your Mail Order Expertise 2. How to Find a Unique Product or Service to Sell 3. How to Make Money with Classified Ads 4. How to Make Money with Display Ads 5. The Unlimited Potential for Making Money with Direct Mail 6. How to Copycat Successful Mail Order Operations 7. How I Created A Best Seller Using the Copycat Technique 8. How to Start and Run a Profitable Mail Order, Special Interest Book or Record Business 9. I Enjoy Selling Books by Mail – Some of My Successful and Not-So-Successful Ads and Direct Mail Circulars 10. Five of My Most Successful Direct Mail Pieces That Sold and Are Still Selling Millions of Dollars Worth of Books 11. Melvin Powers' Mail Order Success Strategy – Follow It and You'll Become a Millionaire 12. How to Sell Your Products to Mail Order Companies, Retail Outlets, Jobbers, and Fund Raisers for Maximum Distribution and Profits 13. How to Get Free Display Ads and Publicity That Can Put You on the Road to Riches 14. How to Make Your Advertising Copy Sizzle to Make You Wealthy 15. Questions and Answers to Help You Get Started Making Money in Your Own Mail Order Business 16. A Personal Word from Melvin Powers 17. How to Get Started Making Money in Mail Order. 18. Selling Products on Television - An Exciting Challenge   8½"x11" – 352 Pages . . . $20.00

HOW TO SELF-PUBLISH YOUR BOOK AND HAVE THE FUN AND EXCITEMENT OF BEING A BEST-SELLING AUTHOR
by Melvin Powers

An expert's step-by-step guide to successfully marketing your book   240 Pages . . . $20.00

A NEW GUIDE TO RATIONAL LIVING
by Albert Ellis, Ph.D. & Robert A. Harper, Ph.D.

1. How Far Can You Go With Self-Analysis? 2. You Feel the Way You Think 3. Feeling Well by Thinking Straight 4. How You Create Your Feelings 5. Thinking Yourself Out of Emotional Disturbances 6. Recognizing and Attacking Neurotic Behavior 7. Overcoming the Influences of the Past 8. Does Reason Always Prove Reasonable? 9. Refusing to Feel Desperately Unhappy 10. Tackling Dire Needs for Approval 11. Eradicating Dire Fears of Failure 12. How to Stop Blaming and Start Living 13. How to Feel Undepressed though Frustrated 14. Controlling Your Own Destiny 15. Conquering Anxiety   256 Pages . . . $10.00

PSYCHO-CYBERNETICS
A New Technique for Using Your Subconscious Power
by Maxwell Maltz, M.D., F.I.C.S.

1. The Self Image: Your Key to a Better Life 2. Discovering the Success Mechanism Within You 3. Imagination – The First Key to Your Success Mechanism 4. Dehypnotize Yourself from False Beliefs 5. How to Utilize the Power of Rational Thinking 6. Relax and Let Your Success Mechanism Work for You 7. You Can Acquire the Habit of Happiness 8. Ingredients of the Success-Type Personality and How to Acquire Them 9. The Failure Mechanism: How to Make It Work For You Instead of Against You 10. How to Remove Emotional Scars, or How to Give Yourself an Emotional Face Lift 11. How to Unlock Your Real Personality 12. Do-It-Yourself Tranquilizers   288 Pages . . . $7.00

A PRACTICAL GUIDE TO SELF-HYPNOSIS
by Melvin Powers

1. What You Should Know About Self-Hypnosis 2. What About the Dangers of Hypnosis? 3. Is Hypnosis the Answer? 4. How Does Self-Hypnosis Work? 5. How to Arouse Yourself from the Self-Hypnotic State 6. How to Attain Self-Hypnosis 7. Deepening the Self-Hypnotic State 8. What You Should Know About Becoming an Excellent Subject 9. Techniques for Reaching the Somnambulistic State 10. A New Approach to Self-Hypnosis When All Else Fails 11. Psychological Aids and Their Function 12. The Nature of Hypnosis 13. Practical Applications of Self-Hypnosis   128 Pages . . . $5.00

The books listed above can be obtained from your book dealer or directly from Melvin Powers. When ordering, please remit $2.00 postage for the first book and $1.00 for each additional book.

Melvin Powers
12015 Sherman Road, No. Hollywood, California 91605